A HISTORY OF
FORT CAMPBELL

JOHN O'BRIEN

THE
History
PRESS

Published by The History Press
Charleston, SC 29403
www.historypress.net

Copyright © 2014 by John O'Brien
All rights reserved

Unless otherwise noted, all images are from the collection of the Don F. Pratt Museum.

First published 2014

Manufactured in the United States

ISBN 978.1.62619.275.1

Library of Congress Control Number: 2014953182

For Colonel Arthur Lombardi*, Colonel Robert Jones* and Colonel Ted Crozier: soldiers, heroes and leading citizens in the growth of the city of Fort Campbell.

*in memoriam

CONTENTS

CONTENTS

CONTENTS

ACKNOWLEDGEMENTS

M uch of the work of historical research takes place in the lonely confines of archives and libraries. In the course of my research in our archives and library, I have had the pleasure to spend time with many hardworking and talented historians who have come before me. I got to know them vicariously through their work, of which this history of the development of the city of Fort Campbell is a synthesis. Captain John Mosher wrote the first history of Fort Campbell in 1952. Clyde Jones expanded on that history in a master's thesis in 1973. Two lieutenants assigned to the Division G3 in 1965, John Jaeger and David Pearson, assembled and drafted a thorough history of Fort Campbell from 1950 through 1965. I have found several marked-up copies of their 190-page draft, but I have yet to find a finished and final copy. I suspect the events surrounding the deployment of the division to Vietnam preempted completion, but even in draft it was a most helpful document. First Lieutenant David Hart wrote a history of the fort and the division in 1978 that provided insight into the United States Army Training Center years, 1967–72. Samiran Chanchani, with whom I did have the pleasure to work in person, assembled an excellent historical context for Fort Campbell during the Cold War years, especially the history of Clarksville Base. Captain Jim Page, a great friend and colleague, left a very complete history of the division in Operation Iraqi Freedom and the Global War on Terror. I am also indebted to the work of colleague and friend Scott Schoner. Scott's work of organizing and digitizing the document and pictorial archives at the Pratt Museum was meticulous and thorough, making access to such records a breeze. The names of numerous other officers who performed the additional duty of division historian, normally a one-year or less assignment, are associated with a large archive and library of Annual Historical Reports and supplements, special studies, replies to historical inquiries and other artifacts of their work that have been essential. To all these, I am indebted.

Fortunately, not all historical research is done in the dark and lonely confines of archives and libraries. Over the years of my association with Fort Campbell as an active-duty officer and as a Department of the Army civilian, I have had the privilege of sharing the daylight and true conviviality with many colleagues, both active-duty military and civilian, who have shared their knowledge and insights about the development of the city. Many of them were not just witnesses but actual participants in the shaping of events. To mention just a few: Jody Jenkins of DPTMS; Director of Contracting Leslie Carrol (who once challenged me that it would not be possible to write a history of the city and thus generated the intellectual curiosity and drive to make this attempt!); Gregory Stallworth of the Equal Opportunity Office and founder of the civilian workforce development program Leadership Fort Campbell; Van Stokes of MWR, "Mr. Outdoor Recreation"; and Helen Zachary and Teresa Mueller of the Strategic Planning Office, who have long plotted and articulated the plan of development for the city for at least a decade of very successful garrison commanders. As a historian, there is a special place in my heart for the engineers on post. If you want to know the physical history of a city, consult the engineer. Master planner Sally Castleman and Deputy Post Engineer Ted Reece, with their insights and with her archive of records, maps and master plans, are wonderful resources for historical inquiry of this kind.

The mission to collect, preserve, interpret and exhibit the history, heritage and values of the city of Fort Campbell and the units that have been assigned is an Army mission that has been greatly enhanced by the moral and financial support of the Fort Campbell Historical Foundation, Inc. The support of the foundation for the historical program, the Don F. Pratt Museum and the future Wings of Liberty Museum is very much a part of the many ways the foundation helps to keep Fort Campbell a "world-class Army home."

A last and heartfelt bit of gratitude must go out to friends and family who encouraged me in this project. Thank you to museum colleagues John Foley, Dan Peterson and Captain Tyler Reid for sharing the research burden and enduring the reading of draft chapters. Thank you to our 2014 Pratt Museum summer intern, Sarah Fry of the Middle Tennessee State

ACKNOWLEDGEMENTS

University graduate program in public history, for proofreading, identifying all those split infinitives and killing passive voice whenever it tried to creep into the manuscript. I owe a special thank-you to my daughter, Bernadette, for her proofreading and insistence on a smooth narrative free of military jargon and "Army speak." Lastly, my most special thank-you goes to my Army bride of thirty-six years, Maria, who has always been the heart and soul of our Army family.

INTRODUCTION

Gate 4, pictured on the back cover, has been the main entrance into Fort Campbell since the camp was constructed in February 1942. The entrance road passes a guard post at Gate 4 and then heads west one mile to the geographic center and highest elevation of the camp. At that spot stands Building T-39, a building that for most of the history of the city of Fort Campbell has served as the combined headquarters for Garrison Command and the headquarters of the commanding general of the major unit assigned to Fort Campbell.

These two iconic features, Gate 4 and T-39, tell us much about the history of Fort Campbell. The "T" associated with a building on an engineer site plan stands for "temporary." This building, T-39, on the site plan for what was conceptually known as the "Tennessee-Kentucky Armor Camp" in 1941 was a division and administration headquarters building of the standard design recently approved by the quartermaster general for Army camps (Type DHQ-1). Every mobilization camp built for World War II had a headquarters administration building of the same design, "one each per camp." The "T" indicated that the service life of the building, like that of the camp itself, was not expected to exceed the length of time it would take to fight and win the war. A maximum service life of five to twenty years was the construction standard for all buildings designed for the mobilization camps.

Now, seventy years later, T-39 still stands and still serves as the headquarters building for the Fort Campbell Garrison Command. It is no small irony that over those many years, almost everyone forgot what the

INTRODUCTION

Building T-39.

"T" stood for. "I'm headed to T-39" became a well-understood euphemism used by subordinate commanders, staff officers and couriers to mean, "I'm headed for the headquarters." One goal of this history is to explain how this temporary mobilization camp built in the "Black Patch" of Tennessee and Kentucky for the Great Crusade of World War II has managed to remain relevant and transform to become the modern city of Fort Campbell. The answer to that question that will unfold in this history is that the decisions made in 1941 to locate the camp here were made for the right reasons. They were decisions based on a set of criteria learned from recent trial and error in the Army mobilization camp construction program. Those who made the decisions were free from inappropriate political interference. The decisions made for the right reasons in 1941 proved enduring, and hence, the camp was adaptable and uniquely suited for continued service as the nation's security needs changed throughout the subsequent decades.

That the Army built its mobilization camps as temporary facilities in 1942 is understandable. There was first and foremost the national tradition and fear against a standing peacetime Army. Secondly, the Army had recently experienced mobilization on a grand scale in support of the Great War in 1917–18. The model used then was to hastily organize units, conduct the briefest of organization and initial stateside training and then ship units to theater as soon as possible for final training and commitment to combat. Stateside facilities to support this model of mobilization were austere, to say the very least. The cantonment area, that part of a camp where the soldiers lived, for those camps consisted of troop housing of ten-man canvas tents stretched over wooden platforms, communal latrines and a mess hall. The drawdown of the Army and the closing of the mobilization camps in the aftermath of that experience taught planners not to get stuck with permanent buildings and facilities at the end of a war. Recalling that over four million men were trained and deployed by this method in the brief twenty months the United States was at war was a testament to the industrial-like efficiency of the system. It did work as a method to raise, train and deploy a mass Army, but it was a ruthlessly impersonal system, and many who had experienced the system as young soldiers themselves in 1917–18 did not want to see it repeated for their sons in 1940–42. The public and politicians would not tolerate the austerity of the Great War mobilization camps for the modern citizen-army of 1940–42, and yet, permanent facilities were out of the question. The dilemma was solved by designers of the Army Quartermaster Corps who developed a plan called the 700 and 800 Series Cantonment Construction Plan. The plan relied on uniform design and modular construction of buildings equipped with all the required modern conveniences. The buildings were made of wood and to a standard allowing for a five- to twenty-year service life. All but two of the hundreds of buildings built at Camp Campbell in 1942 were constructed of wood. The only structures built of material more durable than wood were the magnificent two-thousand-bed Station Hospital built of brick veneer and the water treatment facility built of cement blocks. Even those buildings, however, were identified on the original site plan as no more than "semi-permanent."

Gate 4 is also a visual metaphor for understanding the transition of the camp from temporary to permanent. The cantonment area of the camp was a long, oblong shape that stretched from north to south five miles in length and one and a half miles in width. In city measurements, the length was fifty-six blocks and the width was twelve large blocks. U.S. Highway 41W paralleled the east boundary of the camp along its north–south axis. It was from U.S. 41W that one turned left, if traveling from the south, into Gate 4 and then into the very center of the camp. It was around this center, around T-39, that all official business was conducted. New arrivals, civilian workers, civic leaders, members of voluntary organizations, entertainers, businessmen, contractors, dignitaries and visiting Army officials all passed through Gate 4 to conduct their business. Most importantly, considering the purpose of the camp, it was through Gate 4 that trained units heading for the war in Europe conducted their formal departure. Because of its association with the trip to the center of the camp, Gate 4 soon became, and remains even to this date, the essential and official entrance to the city of Fort Campbell.

With these seventy years of hindsight, it is possible and appropriate to imagine the camp and the fort as always having been one sort of city or another. It has, in fact, been many different kinds of "city." At one time, July 1941–November 1941 for example, it was nothing more than a "conceptual city," a city for soldiers that existed only on the blueprint drawings of Wilson, Bell & Watkins Construction Company. Chapter 1 explains that much political concern and engineering experience went into developing the plans for "city-camps" like Camp Campbell. They did not grow organically like most cities, as in the model of beginning with a gathering of a few settler families that would attract others and multiply over time to grow into a metropolis. Rather, these city-camps were to be constructed and made completely ready for occupation before the first resident arrived. Congress mandated that water, electricity, comfortable barracks, recreation facilities, transportation networks, available labor and a host of considerations be in place before occupation of the first resident. An equally important part of the story of these conceptual city-camps is that they were planned to be built on top of existing rural communities and populations that in the conceptual planning process had to be made and prepared to accept displacement in order to accommodate the new city when built.

Construction of the conceptual city called the Tennessee-Kentucky Armor Camp was authorized 6 January 1942 because of the attack on Pearl Harbor. The city-camp was built between February and September 1942. It was named Camp Campbell on 6 March 1942 and activated on 1 July 1942. The subject of Chapter 2 is the wartime occupation of the city-camp. The 12th Armored Division became the first unit to occupy the camp in September 1942. From September 1942 until March 1948, the "conceptual city" was transformed to become a "giant bachelor city" housing over thirty thousand single or unaccompanied soldiers. There were no accommodations for families. The vast bulk of the drafted citizen Army of World War II was not married and lived by the motto, "If the Army wanted you to have a wife, they would have issued you one." Professional officers and NCOs of the Regular Army assigned to Camp Campbell who were married and brought their families with them had no option but to have their families reside in private residences in nearby Clarksville or Hopkinsville.

With the successful conclusion of World War II and the subsequent demobilization of the Army through 1948, the "giant bachelor city" should have gone away. That was the plan, but there were two big changes in the world that were about to overlap and would change the plan. The first change was the advent of the Cold War; the second was a profound change in military sociology wherein the new postwar Army "got married." The first change, the Cold War, would bring about the need for the nation to develop and maintain a nuclear arsenal and, at least initially, reverse the steep drawdown of the Army and build a large, mostly drafted and standing peacetime Army. For all the same reasons that Camp Campbell made for an excellent location for a mobilization camp in 1941, so, too, did those reasons lead to the decision to build "Site Charlie," one of the thirteen top-secret nuclear storage sites constructed across the United States from 1948 to 1952. Site Charlie was built within Camp Campbell and tethered to the existing infrastructure. It was named Clarksville Base. With the decision to build Clarksville Base, a facility that housed about one-third of the nation's nuclear arsenal, came the decision to station in near proximity an active-duty army division at the old camp. Thus it was that the old camp, in a rather decrepit state in 1948, was rescued from oblivion. The 11th Airborne Division, on occupation duty in Japan since the end of the war, was transferred to Camp Campbell in 1948. The status of the temporary camp was upgraded to that of a permanent fort in April 1950. In Chapter 3, it will be explained how the new Fort Campbell transformed to become a new kind of city, a "national defense city," of the early Cold War. Many new facilities were required to accommodate a large, married, peacetime Army, not the least of which were permanent quarters for single soldiers and family housing and schools for married soldiers. A very distinctive and still visible Cold War architecture to accommodate the nuclear base, the peacetime Army and a married Army was added to the landscape of the city.

The nature of the Cold War changed in the early 1960s, and the rumblings of a new transition for the city could be felt. The Soviets saw an advantage in sponsoring proxy wars or wars of national liberation. These low-intensity wars required something less than a full nuclear response. Under President Kennedy, a new national strategy of "flexible response" required the Army to reorganize and transform its war fighting doctrine to address the "full spectrum of conflict." Counterinsurgency, low-intensity conflict and conventional response to less than nuclear threats were capabilities added to the Army's war fighting doctrine. The first big test and application of this new doctrine came in Vietnam. In July 1965, the 1st Brigade of the 101st Airborne Division deployed to Vietnam. Twenty-six months later, in January 1968, the remainder of the division followed the 1st Brigade to Vietnam. In Chapter 4, we will see how the character and the nature of the city transformed once again to accommodate new circumstances. When the 101st Airborne Division departed Fort Campbell, it departed *in toto*. There was no such thing back then as a rear detachment. The break with the fort was complete, clean and permanent. In a very awkward moment in Army history, 101st Airborne Division families were required to move out of family quarters because Fort Campbell was no longer their home. In place of the 101st Airborne Division, the Army established a training center at Fort Campbell. To reflect its new mission, the formal name of the city became "the United States Army Training Center and Fort Campbell, Kentucky." Fort Campbell transformed to become a "Basic Training City" composed of a small garrison staff, the hospital, a reception station, a brigade-sized unit called the Combat Arms Group (Provisional) and two basic training brigade cadres of drill sergeants who shepherded over 248,000 basic trainees through ten-week basic training cycles from 1968 to 1972. The change in 1968 had a profound economic and cultural effect on the surrounding communities as the stable Army families of an active-duty division were replaced by transitory, young, single, male soldiers undergoing their initial basic training in the Army.

The long war in Vietnam was brought to a close for the 101st Airborne Division in April–May 1972. Chapter 5 begins with the closing of the U.S. Army Training Center at Fort Campbell and the very real concern that the 101st Airborne Division (Airmobile) would not necessarily return from Vietnam to Fort Campbell. There was a strong possibility that the fort would be closed. The possibility that the 101st might not return to Fort Campbell was because when the division departed in 1968, it was organized and equipped as a paratrooper division. In Vietnam, it had been reorganized as an airmobile division. It was now equipped with hundreds more aircraft needing airfields and maintenance facilities and the addition of hundreds more warrant officers who flew those hundreds of helicopters. The warrant officers were authorized officer family housing. The problem was that the old home of the 101st required much in the way of a facilities upgrade to house this new kind of division. Congress very nearly made the Army station the 101st Airborne Division (Airmobile) at Fort Stewart, Georgia, because nearby Hunter Army Airfield could have accommodated the large helicopter fleet. A hard-fought battle led by civic leaders in Clarksville, however, resulted in Congress relenting and allowing the Army to return the division to Fort Campbell after all. This stationing decision set in motion the intensive planning, budget allocation and building program that would be required to upgrade the city.

As the facilities to support the housing, training and material needs of an airmobile division were taking shape, two other fundamental changes within the Army occurred that affected the character of the city and caused it to transform again. Chapter 6 highlights the underlying forces that drove a new transformation of the city. First, Congress and Army leadership decided to end the draft-era Army of 1948–72 and replace it with an all-volunteer force. The acronym VOLAR (Volunteer Army) described a host of programs to upgrade and make professional Army life. Dovetailing with the VOLAR transition was the Army of Excellence (AOE) initiative. The quest to end the malaise brought about by the Vietnam experience and the startling and frightening impact of the 1973 Arab-Israeli War spurred Army leadership to develop new training concepts, advanced weaponry, new war fighting doctrine and organization to meet the modern Soviet threat, especially in Europe. These initiatives were backed and funded by the Reagan administration through the 1980s. The effect of these initiatives on the city of Fort Campbell was profound. The new type of city and civic management philosophy that emerged from this transformation was called the Army Community of Excellence (ACOE). Army leadership was determined that a professional military career in the VOLAR/AOE must include the amenities of a comfortable and fulfilling life on par with that enjoyed by the civilian community contemporaries of young soldiers and officers. In the words of the deputy post commander at the time, Colonel Art Lombardi, "We are involved in an effort to humanize the Army." The effect of ACOE initiatives and funding for modernization on the city were startling. Hardly anything new had been added to the architecture of the city during the Vietnam years, but millions and millions of dollars in new construction were programmed during the 1980s and '90s to meet the VOLAR/AOE goals, provide a much-needed facelift and add a whole new layer—a visually distinct layer—of infrastructure of the city.

As the 1990s began, while in full stride of the ACOE improvements, the Soviet Union collapsed, resulting in the end of the Cold War. This dramatic change in the international strategic environment, and the spectacular performance of the Army in the Gulf War in 1990–91 that validated the VOLAR and AOE programs, ushered in a new chapter of the history of the city of Fort Campbell. A new mission, or purpose, in the 1990s became "to deploy and sustain expeditionary forces." In its doctrine, the Army turned from a focus on the Cold War adversary of the Soviet Union and began to consider Military Operations Other than War, or MOOTW. The MOOTW operations carried out by Fort Campbell units throughout the 1990s involved a variety of small-unit, limited-duration deployments with a purpose "less than war." Peacekeeping in the Sinai, peace enforcement in Bosnia and Somalia, disaster response in Central America and low-intensity operations short of war like in Haiti, enforcement of the no-fly zones in Iraq, etc., were the new paradigm. The term "power projection platform" was used in a starkly utilitarian meaning by military planners to describe the new purpose of the city. What was required to meet the needs of the Army was a significant upgrade to deployment facilities and infrastructure. Millions of construction program dollars funded rail loading and interchange yard upgrades, airfield and passenger terminal area construction and over-the-road transport upgrades.

The experience of Operations Desert Shield/Desert Storm revealed more than just deployment and infrastructure facility shortcomings. An honest and thorough assessment in the aftermath of the Gulf War revealed that even though the VOLAR/AOE Army performed magnificently on the battlefield, there were shortcomings on the homefront, in the heart of the city, of a less tangible but equally important nature. There was a weakness within the Army family at home station. As the soldiers deployed, many families, including those of senior officers and noncommissioned officers, chose to ride out the uncertainty of the deployment away from Fort Campbell with their extended families. Recognizing the adverse impact, especially for young Army families, and cognizant of the fact that frequent and unpredictable deployments by the expeditionary units at Fort Campbell were the new reality, the Army addressed this issue throughout the 1990s by building a program of Family Readiness Groups (FRGs). FRG training for commanders and senior noncommissioned officers and their spouses was augmented by building the types of facilities and services within the city designed to support and sustain the well-being of the families of an expeditionary Army. The Gulf War exodus of family in 1990–91 also had an extreme effect on the economies of the neighboring communities of Clarksville, Hopkinsville and Oak Grove. So severe was the impact that both the U.S. Department of Commerce and the U.S. Department of Labor conducted surveys to assess the negative consequences on the local economy. In tandem with the development of the FRG program, civic leaders from the surrounding communities joined with commanders and their families at Fort Campbell to foster deeper relations between Army families and the local community.

The efforts to rebuild the Army as a modern, professional and expeditionary force in the 1980s and 1990s had a synergistic effect with the blending of efforts to build an Army community that provided for a rewarding career. Mission readiness and family well-being were now recognized as essential priorities—not as competing and opposite ends of the mission and funding spectrum—in building a successful Army. The current chapter of the city's history is how the city adopted the philosophy and motto, "A World-Class Army Home." The wisdom of this approach met the severest of tests on 11 September 2001. Since that hideous attack, the Army and Army families have been faced with a decade of persistent conflict in the Global War on Terror (GWOT). Long deployments, family separations, battlefield losses and debilitating wounds could have brought down a lesser force, lesser families and a lesser nation.

When I began contemplating this project in 2003, I asked friends and associates if they thought it possible to consider the fort as a city and, if so, as a city with a history of its own, separate from the military units assigned to the fort. To my surprise, the consensus at the time was no to both. Dissenters objected that it would be nothing more than a quaint literary device to conflate a real Army fort with that of a city, as they also objected to the idea of the fort being anything more than a subset of the history of the unit in residence. While I do concede their point that without soldiers there cannot be an Army camp or fort, I have come to the conclusion, nonetheless, that there is a distinct civic history of this camp and fort that is discernible in the voices of soldiers and their family members when they say, "Fort Campbell is my home." With all due respect to my friends and associates, I believe their initial response to the question in 2003 was shortsighted. We were at that time caught in the immediacy of a historical moment that may have clouded our better reflection. We were supporting and sustaining all the units at Fort Campbell deployed to operations in Afghanistan and Iraq. Our purpose in that moment was to act as a strategic "power projection platform" for deployed Army forces. Perhaps a little more hidden at that moment were the more than fifty-eight thousand family members who continued to reside in what certainly looked and acted like a city. Secondly, we were in that time focused on the units assigned to Fort Campbell and may have temporarily lost the longer view that many other units had made a similar journey from the camp or the fort to a theater of war: the 26th Infantry Division and the

12th, 14th and 20th Armored Divisions of World War II; the 187th Airborne Regimental Combat Team of 11th Airborne Division in Korea; the 101st Airborne to Vietnam and Saudi Arabia; and other deployments in the busy 1990s. Army units come and go, and yet the city remains. Lastly, and perhaps most importantly, it is the purpose of this history to answer the curiosity of new residents, the thousands of family members and soldiers who rotate through the city every year, when they see in any panoramic view of their city the jumble of distinct architecture representing eras gone by and ask, "What happened here?" They are asking, in essence, that quintessential historical question that demands an answer: "What is the history of my hometown?" For those who live and work here, this is the story of how your hometown became the city of Fort Campbell.

CHAPTER 1

INCREMENTAL MOBILIZATION AND THE RISE OF THE GIANT CITY-CAMPS

THE CONCEPTUAL CITY

The world went to war in 1939. The United States did not. It took the horrific and unprecedented attack on Pearl Harbor on 7 December 1941 to "waken the giant." What is now the vibrant city of Fort Campbell had its birth in this period, 1939–41. When the unwanted war came, the United States found itself woefully unprepared. Many factors explain this state of unpreparedness, including the disappointing calamity of the Great War that failed to "make the world safe for democracy" only twenty years prior and a resurgence of a tradition of American neutrality. Another factor was the brutal economic reality of a Great Depression that would not be tamed and that was growing worse in the latter years of the 1930s. In the competition for limited national resources between "preparedness and guns" or "peace and butter," it was "butter" that was more often than not the winner. The country was bitterly and almost evenly divided between advocates for preparedness and advocates for neutrality. The state of the Army at the beginning of 1939 reflected this divided vision. It was the product of an isolationist plan for strategic defense requiring a very small force, equipped and trained with a war fighting doctrine from the previous war and inadequate logistical plans for expansion, if required.

U.S. military strategy in the 1920s and '30s favored disengagement and detachment from the affairs of other nations. It was based on the concept of Hemispheric Defense.[1] This was a passive strategy that relied on the isolation of the U.S. mainland provided by the Pacific and Atlantic Oceans. The role of the Army, and hence the size of the Army and National Guard, was tailored to defend the coasts from foreign invasion and to defend overseas territories and possessions. In 1939, the size of the Army was 187,893 officers and soldiers. One-fourth of the force, about 50,000 officers and soldiers, was assigned to the overseas territories (Panama, Philippines, Alaska and Hawaii). The remaining 137,000 officers and soldiers assigned stateside were dispersed among 130 mostly battalion-sized posts (600 personnel) spread across the United States but mostly located in the Midwest and western states in locations that only sixty years previously had been sited to support the wars against the Plains Indians.[2] Even back then, congressmen found it difficult to give up the economic benefits of a military installation located within their district.

The backup to the very small Regular Army was the National Guard. In 1939, the National Guard was organized between the forty-eight states into eighteen under-strength divisions. National Guard manpower was slightly larger than that of the Regular Army, about 200,000 men. Training for the National Guard consisted of a mere forty-eight training days and one two-week field exercise per year. National Guard training locations seldom were large enough to accommodate larger than company- or battalion-sized units. Although the National Guard units were a "force in being," it was no secret that the Guard would require extensive training before it could even remotely be considered combat ready.[3]

The Army of late 1939 was a small, outdated and ill-equipped force. The basic equipment and armament of the Regular Army and the National Guard through the 1930s was Great War (1917–18) vintage. The basic artillery piece was the French 75mm gun, though a much more capable 105mm howitzer had been developed. The basic infantry rifle was the dependable bolt-action Springfield rifle, though the semi-automatic M1 Garand was designed and in limited production. The vintage (and highly inaccurate) three-inch Stokes mortar remained in field use, though the new Brandt-Stokes 60mm and 81mm mortars were developed and ready for production. The Army was seriously deficient in heavier and more modern equipment. Modern radios and signal equipment, tanks, anti-tank guns and antiaircraft weapons were not in production and, worse, were not yet even in design.

Even more problematic, the Army of 1939 lacked a doctrinal and organizational strategy for fighting a modern war. Between 1939 and 1941, the United States witnessed the awesome technological advancements in aircraft, tanks and airborne forces that characterized a new type of warfare being fought in Europe called Blitzkrieg or Lightning War. Combat film footage of the German invasions of Belgium, Holland, Poland and France demonstrated the striking power of the combination of modern bomber aircraft, air-delivered soldiers and the unimaginable power of mechanized divisions made of armadas of armored vehicles. The visual spectacle witnessed in Saturday afternoon matinee newsreels stunned Americans by the sheer depth and breadth of modern industrial warfare. By contrast, the pictures and newsreels of our Army taken during the Louisiana Maneuvers of 1940 showed our soldiers in World War I vintage uniforms behind wooden replica machine guns made of broomsticks and on jeeps with placards that said "tank." Those images remind us of just how unprepared the Army of 1939 was for modern war.[4]

The War Department made plans for the expansion of this small force in the 1930s. The plan was called the Protective Mobilization Plan, or PMP. The mobilization plans were based on the World War I model of rapid expansion and commitment to combat as soon as possible. These plans envisioned the construction of austere camps, the troop housing provided being mostly ten-man canvas tents pulled over rough wood frames and/ or warehouses converted to temporary dormitories. In keeping with the World War I experience, these camps would be adequate for a short period of initial training before the unit would be shipped overseas to conduct final training and then employment in combat. If subsequent units were activated, they, in turn, would occupy the recently vacated temporary camp and facilities to begin their short period of initial organization and training before deployment. The process could be repeated in many places and as often as necessary.[5]

When the world went to war in September 1939, the strategic calculus in the War Department necessarily began to change. Isolationism as a strategy, though still strongly supported by nearly half the population, was fast becoming untenable. With the president's direction, a series of "Rainbow Plans" was carefully crafted and developed that addressed how the United States would respond to contingencies and combinations of contingencies against multiple foes outside the western hemisphere. In all these contingencies, strategic planners visualized an M-Day (Mobilization Day) that would mark the clear end of peace and the beginning of war. But because there was no clear or compelling cause to declare an M-Day in 1939–41, mobilization plans remained just that—plans. There were, however, continual, increasing and ominous global threats. While not enough to trigger an M-Day, these

Camp Wheeler, Georgia, 1917. *U.S. Army photo.*

threats did lead to a limited, grudging and compromise-riddled expansion of the existing Army and Navy, especially after the fall of France in June 1940. In what became a compromise between those who feared the inevitability of the United States being dragged into the global turmoil in an unprepared state and those who feared waste of precious resources and unnecessary provocation of potential enemies, the United States met threats and took limited preparedness steps on an ad hoc basis that came to be called, after the fact, "incremental mobilization." Incremental mobilization described those prudent but politically acceptable steps toward better preparation in a dangerous world that were significantly less than triggering the full mobilization of the M-Day plan. This phenomenon of incremental mobilization attempted to fix the dangers and deficiencies of the pre-1939 Army but without bringing the country to a full war footing.[6]

When the "Phony War" in Europe came to an end in June 1940, the period of incremental mobilization began. This lasted for eighteen months and ended with the attack at Pearl Harbor on 7 December 1941 and a Declaration of War that singled the full mobilization of all the nation's resources envisioned by the politically illusive M-Day. Given the circumstances in Europe and the Far East in June 1940, the continuation of mere war planning was inadequate; tangible preparedness steps were required. For the Army, those important steps included an increase in manpower, modernization and the implied requirement to build a stateside troop cantonment system to house and train the expanding and modernizing Army. The results of this effort were remarkable. In the eighteen months between June 1940 and December 1941, the Army expanded from 210,000 men to 1.6 million men on active duty. Among many modernization improvements, the Armor Forces Command and five completely new and unique armor divisions were organized. The military construction program that was devised to house and train the expanding and modernizing Army built sixty-one temporary "city-camps" that housed all but 270,000 of the 1.6 million men mobilized up to that time.

These eighteen months of incremental mobilization were not without flaw. Temptation at local and state level to take advantage of so much government money being spent in emergency circumstances was real. In many cases, inexperience in construction management, political corruption and cronyism and even plain incompetence plagued the start-up. Many lessons were learned, however, and many corrections were applied. The city of Fort Campbell was conceived and planned during the latter part of this period of incremental mobilization, July–November 1941. Those planners were the beneficiaries of the lessons learned, and they applied those lessons well.

The first incremental step undertaken was to expand the size of the Army. President Roosevelt issued an Executive Order in June 1940 that increased the Regular Army by 17,000 and increased the National Guard by 100,000. The president declared a "limited state of emergency." In light of the state of emergency, the president asked Congress to authorize and fund federalizing the National Guard. Congress passed that legislation in August but, as the problem with compromise between preparedness advocates and neutrality advocates would have it throughout the period of incremental measures, with certain limitations. The National Guard would be federalized for one year but only for the purpose of training. Further, the National Guard units were not to be employed in combat anywhere outside the western hemisphere. Under a great deal of pressure from preparedness lobbyists, Congress also prepared an additional piece of legislation, the Burke-Wadsworth Bill, known as the Selective Service Act of 1940. The Selective Service Act was profound in that for the first time in our nation's history, a peacetime draft and a "standing army" of significant size was authorized. The Selective Service Act called for an initial surge of 400,000 draftees, expanding up to 700,000 more within a year. As with the legislation authorizing the federalizing of the National Guard, the Selective Service Act came with strings attached. Draftees were not to be employed outside the western hemisphere either, but more significantly, the act specified housing requirements for the draftee Army. Congress made it explicit that the citizen-soldiers of the new draftee Army would not live in the "tents and mess hall" environment of the World War I Army: "snug barracks, toilets, showers, heating, and electric lights," it was stipulated, would have to be in place before these new soldiers arrived at camps, which at this time had hardly even been conceptualized.[7]

Ambitious expansion required generous funding. Munitions plants and seacoast defenses were very high priorities, but troop housing was the most pressing upfront need. Congress passed four supplemental budget authorizations in 1940–41 providing a staggering $128 million earmarked specifically for a military construction program. As is often the case when immediate demand and large government appropriations collide, there is opportunity for graft, corruption, cronyism and plain old-fashioned incompetence. Such was the case with the Army construction program, especially in the initial effort to house the mobilized National Guard units. Mistakes were made, and there was a public outcry. Poor site selection due to cronyism and political interference, inadequate engineer surveys and lack of attention to transportation requirements had led to construction delays and cost overruns of $28 million at Camp Blanding, Florida; Indiantown Gap, Pennsylvania; and Camp Leonard Wood, Missouri. In response, a Senate Special Committee to Investigate the National Defense Program was established in March 1941 to investigate corruption and make recommendations concerning national defense spending. The committee was headed by Senator Harry Truman (D) of Missouri and came to be called the Truman Committee. By the end of the war, the Truman Committee had proven to be one of the most successful oversight committees in Senate history. Cost overruns, mismanagement and political interference related to the construction of military camps and cantonments were the first targets of the committee. The committee laid down a series of recommendations that, in essence, freed the Army from political interference in site selection and streamlined construction management by merging the Quartermaster Construction Division and the Corps of Engineer Construction Division. The survey and construction of Camp Campbell took place in July–November 1941, well after the Truman Committee recommendations had been implemented. In other words, Camp Campbell planning and construction was done in an environment where the scrutiny and popularity of the Truman Committee eliminated by both peer and public pressure the temptation for politicians to interfere with the best interests of the Army in the construction program.[8]

With expansion underway, modernization of the force was the next most pressing need. The crushing of Poland and France by a modern German army using large-scale mechanized forces and a new war fighting doctrine called Blitzkrieg was frightening and alarming. Much needed to be brought up to date, including the organization of infantry divisions, antiaircraft artillery, amphibious capability, the organization of tank destroyer elements and the use of airborne troops. Developing an armored force to take on the Germans, however, became a first priority. Army General Headquarters (GHQ) established a new command, the Armored Forces Command (AFC), to bring the stagnant U.S. Army of World War I into the age of modern armored warfare. Brigadier General Adna Chaffee was appointed the first chief of the new command. The new command was headquartered at Fort Knox, Kentucky. Brigadier General Chaffee was made responsible for all phases of the development, organizing and training of an armored force. Fort Knox became the home of the Armored Force School, Armor Officer Candidate School (OCS), the Armor Board and the Armored Force Replacement Training Center. Within weeks, the new command had formed the first two Armored Divisions from existing cavalry, infantry and artillery units (1st Armored Division, Fort Knox, and 2nd Armored Division, Fort Benning). Three more armored divisions (3rd AD, 4th AD and 5th AD) were organized within the year and were training at Camp Beauregard, Louisiana (now Fort Polk); Pine Camp, New York (now Fort Drum); and Camp Cooke, California (now Vandenberg Air Force Base). The AFC learned what was required to house and train an armored division.[9] The training and maintenance needs of the new armored divisions were vastly beyond that of a standard infantry division. Increased maintenance and repair facilities were mandatory, as well as larger maneuver areas for combined arms formations and enhanced ranges for the armor division components of tanks, mechanized infantry and armored field artillery. This information was of the upmost importance if and when new armor training camps went into survey and planning. When an armored camp was to be planned and surveyed for the Hopkinsville, Kentucky area in November 1942, an AFC officer, First Lieutenant J.G. Junius, was added to the survey and planning team.

Housing this expanding and modernizing Army was itself a monumental task. Prior to 1940, there was not a plan to house a peacetime Army. The 1938–39 PMPs were based on the World War I model. Planners were convinced there was no need for an extensive troop housing and construction

The Army team that oversaw the survey. *Left to right*: Captain Wysong, Lieutenant Junius and Major Retter.

program. The Army had to scramble to develop a housing plan that would meet the stringent demands that Congress had built into legislation for housing a peacetime Army of citizen soldiers.

The Army Quartermaster Corps Construction Division rose to the occasion. The head of the division, Colonel Charles D. Hartman, with a small staff of eighty architects and draftsmen, cobbled together a set of construction plans radically different in purpose and design from that of the PMP. The new plan was called the 700 Series Plan. The plan provided a general site plan for the new camps and the detailed blueprints and construction diagrams for over three hundred assorted and standardized structures that could be used to assemble a camp. The most ubiquitous of the standardized structures was the two-story troop barracks, Plan No. 700-1165. The 700 Series Plan was updated in late 1941 to the Series 800 Plan. Camp Campbell was constructed on the Series 800 Plan.

Because of this standardization of plans, organizing and building a cantonment area on a camp followed a very logical process. The starting point was a company-sized housing echelon area of six buildings. The six buildings of a company echelon were three of the two-story troop barracks,

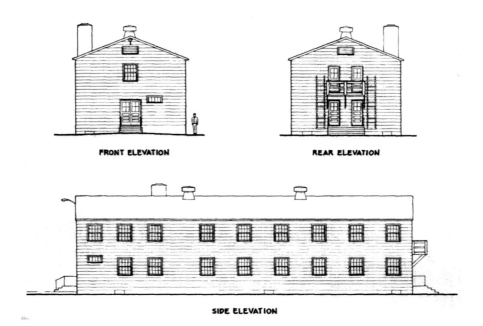

FRONT ELEVATION

REAR ELEVATION

SIDE ELEVATION

one mess hall, one storehouse/orderly room and one recreation building. Three sets of company echelons, plus the additional buildings authorized to a battalion housing echelon, made a battalion housing area echelon. Three sets of battalion housing area echelons, plus the additional buildings authorized to a regimental housing area echelon, made a regimental housing area echelon, and so on until a division-sized cantonment area with all ancillary buildings and facilities for managing a camp were in place:

> *Six buildings completed the company group—three barracks, a mess hall, a storehouse and a recreation building. Six company units are placed together to form a regiment group which include (in addition to the company buildings) headquarters administration buildings, infirmary, chapel, barracks for the headquarters company, regimental cold storage building, truck garage and fire house. Regimental groups are separate from each other by 250-ft. open strips as a fire break.* [10]

The logic of building a cantonment from a company-sized echelon up was immensely helpful to civilian construction firms bidding for contracts. From knowing the type and organization of unit that was to occupy the planned camp, civilian architects and civil engineers could easily lay out the configuration of the cantonment on the selected terrain, estimate the material required from the type and number of buildings to be constructed, estimate labor and estimate cost.[11]

The issue of comfort for the soldiers of the citizen army was from the beginning of incremental mobilization an uncompromising public concern, but it rose to the level of presidential politics in the election of 1940. The Republican candidate, Wendell Willkie, made a campaign accusation that the camps would not be adequate or even ready for the troops as they came into service, to which President Roosevelt responded and promised, "I can give assurance to the mothers and fathers of America that each and every one of their boys in training will be well housed." The president's wife, Eleanor Roosevelt, served as co-chair of the influential Advisory Commission to the Council of National Defense (NDAC). The council addressed the aesthetic and moral aspects of the camp construction. It was by her influence that the new wood construction would be painted and not left bare; that chapels would not be merely utilitarian rectangles but would have a steeple and a church-like appearance reminiscent of home; and that wherever possible, the layout of the camp would have curved roads—curvilinear design, as it was called—to break the stark appearance of regimentation.[12]

The size and scope of these giant city-camps of 1941 were a far cry indeed from the austere "tent cities" envisioned by the 1939 PMP. In conveniences, functions and even in some ways in appearance, these camps were, in fact, small cities unto themselves, often even dwarfing neighboring civilian cities. In his Annual Report of 1941, Secretary of War Henry Stimson summed the accomplishment:

> *A program of construction involving the construction of over 40 veritable cities qualified to receive a minimum of 10,000 to a maximum of 60,000 inhabitants and entertaining all the necessary utilities and conveniences including recreation buildings, theaters, service clubs, chapels, athletic areas, hospitals, bakeries, laundries and cold storage plants, was carried through on time and with a minimum of hardship on the troops.*

By June 1941, the initial manpower goals of incremental mobilization were being met. A total of 1.6 million men had been drafted, mobilized and housed. Those favoring preparedness had pushed the country about as far as was politically possible. There came a significant political push-back from those who favored a policy of strict neutrality. Powerful and vocal organizations such as the America First movement and a very visible opposition to ROTC departments on college campuses highlighted the strength of popular discontent. Money became tighter. Although construction momentum came to an end about June 1941, planning now had to be done on a very constricted budget. Many in the Army saw an inevitable wartime personnel expansion of up to 8 million men and more city-camps to come. Though funds for construction and toleration for continued preparations had come to a trickle by June 1941, a great momentum of experience and knowledge—military and civilian contractor alike—was prepared to surge forward if and when circumstances demanded. After extensive input from his field commanders, the new chief of the Quartermaster Construction Division, Brigadier General Brehon Somervell, recommended to Army Chief of Staff General George C. Marshall six locations in May and then fourteen more locations in July for future city-camps. Somervell advocated for an "advance planning project." He envisioned that twenty-one camps would be required to house the next and inevitable increment of personnel expansion, if preparedness advocates had their way, assumed to bring the peacetime Army strength up to 3 million men. The Army had played hard to catch up with housing for the first peacetime draft and mobilization. Somervell did not want to fall behind again. General Marshall agreed with the plan and approved the locations. With what limited funds were available for construction planning in late 1941, he authorized preliminary surveys and construction planning. No funds in late 1941 were available for land acquisition or construction. One of those locations approved in July was known on paper as the Tennessee-Kentucky Armor Camp. It was to be located in the vicinity of Clarksville, Tennessee, and Hopkinsville, Kentucky.[13] The survey was conducted between August and November 1941, and it caused a big stir in the local area. When it was completed on 15 November 1941, it was put on the shelf, awaiting further international developments. As the plan went on the shelf, no one in America knew that far off in the Pacific near Yokohama, Japan, a Japanese carrier attack force weighed anchor en route to Hawaii...

CHAPTER 2

FROM SITE SELECTION TO CAMP CONSTRUCTION

SITE SELECTION

Much myth and lore surrounds the story of how the site for the Tennessee-Kentucky Armor Camp came to be selected. Was the decision purely political, the result of chicanery and pressure exerted by politicians with a vested interest? Or was the decision strictly utilitarian, with nothing other than the best interest of the Army in consideration? Trying to sort the answer to that question from the evidence provided in the local press or from sterile Army mobilization history can be a bit confusing and lead to erroneous conclusions. Local papers tended to rely on local politicians as a source for their stories. Such sources may have been tempted to embellish their own role and importance in the matter, reinforced, one can only imagine, by local "tavern talk." The Army's official history of mobilization is stiff and lacks any local color. The truth, however, as was the case with almost all of the giant city-camps built for World War II, is that there was a little bit of both the sincere political booster and the tough, analytical staff officer who participated in the decision-making process, albeit with the final decision being very heavily weighted in favor of the latter.

As enthusiasm for preparedness had waned considerably by June 1941, funds for continued personnel expansion and camp construction dried up. The Army, however, continued to plan and even managed to squeeze enough funds, about $95 million, from Congress in the fiscal year (FY) 1941

Army appropriation authorization to do a limited number of site surveys for possible future camp locations. The 1.6 million men on active duty, although a considerable number, were substantially fewer than the War Planning Department's new calculation of 6 million men required to win a global war, if it should come to that. The calculation of 6 million men was not just a raw end strength number; it factored the force structure and the types of units required, of which armored divisions were still a very key consideration. For those planners anticipating construction of additional camps for a next increment of personnel mobilization, it was assumed that eighteen camps for infantry divisions and two camps for armored divisions would be required somewhat immediately to house the new conscription.[14] With a solid construction program, a well-developed staff and proven procedures in being, the Army "leaned forward in the saddle," so to speak, to be ready for the eventuality.

As the camp construction program progressed into 1941, early deficiencies were corrected and standard planning procedures were adopted. From the Army staff perspective, the G3 (training and operations) developed a list of desirable criteria to support training and designated general geographical areas where it would be advantageous to locate new camps. The G4 (logistics) established criteria for construction, such as speed of construction, available labor, supply of material, transportation networks and the like. The consolidated criteria of what the Army staff was looking for were distributed to the quartermaster general. The quartermaster general had divided the forty-eight states into nine zones of construction and appointed a commander, usually a colonel or lieutenant colonel, as a zone commander of each. The nine zone commanders supervised and managed ongoing construction within their zones and were now also charged to search for new camp locations based on the Army staff criteria. As data was gathered, the zone commanders designated a board consisting of an engineer officer, a medical officer, a construction quartermaster and a line officer representing the type of unit for which a camp was being selected to review and assess the data. The boards were authorized to conduct field reconnaissance, if required. It was their purpose to nominate and prioritize potential locations within their zones for campsites that met the Army staff criteria. By May 1941, the zones had identified 250 possible camp locations. Board results were consolidated at the Army Quartermaster Construction Division. The chief of that division, Brigadier General Brehon Somervell, and his staff worked the consolidated nominations into a final prioritized list presented to the chief of staff of the Army, General George C. Marshall. General

Marshall presented the final recommendation to the secretary of the Army, Henry L. Stimson, who personally approved the final site selections for FY 1941 on 16 July 1941.[15]

To understand how local politicians and boosters influenced the very high-level decision-making process for site selection, we must go back to June 1940, when the ad hoc incremental mobilization process began. In essence, preparedness was a large national government program that represented an opportunity for state and local governments to attract federal dollars to their areas for economic development. The practice of local politicians and boosters attracting government or private enterprise to their local areas was not new, was not inherently corrupt and most certainly was not unfamiliar to chambers of commerce, city councils and similar public and private civic institutions. One might even suggest that since the early 1800s the practice had been a distinctly American tradition and one greatly enhanced in the decade of the 1930s, when government work projects were a key ingredient of the New Deal economic recovery programs.

In the context of the times, the 1920s was a time when boosterism became prevalent across America as a means of local economic development. It was a time, as President Calvin Coolidge said, when "the business of America is business." Boosters were citizens belonging to private sector organizations like the chamber of commerce who would actively court and entice entrepreneurs and enterprises to locate to the represented area by touting the benefits offered. Boosters and politicians attracting a railroad to build a line to a given town would be an example of boosterism on the large scale. The Depression and New Deal programs of the 1930s added a political dimension to the practice of boosterism by locating the effort within the political system rather than in the private sector. Programs such as the Civilian Conservation Corps (CCC), the Public Works Administration (PWA) and the Work Projects Administration (WPA) were the sources of nomination for projects, and the flow of federal dollars routed predominantly through political channels. The largest example of a federal program in the Clarksville-Hopkinsville area was that of the Tennessee Valley Authority (TVA), which had recently employed ten thousand men in the building of Lake Barkley and Kentucky Lake. The project provided for rural electrification throughout western Kentucky and Tennessee.

The first and most sustained and successful effort to attract the Army to the local area seems to have come from the Hopkinsville Chamber of Commerce, which began its efforts early in July–August 1940 just as incremental mobilization was getting underway. The chamber promoted use of an eighteen-thousand-acre federal game preserve known today as the Pennyrile State Park, located seventeen miles north of town, as a camp. From a booster perspective, offering the location would yield many economic benefits in return. Aside from the large construction crew and soldier payroll, the certainty of paving the graveled road Kentucky Highway 109, also known as the Dawson Springs Road, between Hopkinsville and the campsite would connect Hopkinsville to the Outwood Hospital, located about halfway between the town and the proposed campsite. A modern black-topped road had been a long-sought local improvement.[16]

Efforts in Clarksville were slower to start and tended to rely more on local government efforts than that of boosters. The slower start is understandable. It took time for the Army to develop channels through which politicians could recognize and then effectively lobby the system. A larger problem, however, was that Clarksville had no large public acreage, such as the federal game preserve, with which to tempt the Army. Acreage in the local area was privately owned farms. Tempting the Army with other people's private property was problematic for local politicians. Enthusiasm for a camp was muted in Clarksville until after the Army made the site selection announcement in July 1941, at which time a sense of patriotic inevitability provided cover for politicians. A host of new and lucrative government programs were developed to aid with substantial dollars the famers who were dislocated and to offer funds to local communities that would necessarily have to expand community infrastructure to accommodate the large, federally mandated construction crew and soldier population.[17]

The intersection of Army needs and the hopes of civilian boosters/politicians occurred in the spring of 1941, when the officer board considering camp locations at the Zone 5 Quartermaster Construction Division (Columbus, Ohio) dispatched a reconnaissance team to Hopkinsville to further assess the federal game preserve proposal. The team was looking for suitable terrain for an armor camp. The game preserve offered by the Hopkinsville boosters was much too small (eighteen thousand acres versus a desired seventy-five thousand acres), and it was also very hilly with steep crags that made it unsuitable for tracked vehicle training. While the team was in the Hopkinsville area, however, it did have the opportunity to visit and assess the much more favorable terrain in south Christian County in the vicinity of the small town of La Fayette, Kentucky (just north of what was to become Camp Campbell). The gently rolling farm terrain to the south and east along the border between Tennessee and Kentucky caught the eye of the team because it was very favorable for armor maneuver and offered good possibilities for development of a cantonment area. As important as the favorable terrain was, more importantly, the team sensed and reported that "local sentiment in favor of a camp was very positive." This positive sentiment seems to have been almost the most important discovery the reconnaissance uncovered.[18]

Newspaper articles from Hopkinsville (17 June and 28 July 1941) and Clarksville (29 July 1941) highlighted some of those analytical Army criteria that were applied to the local area. The proposed location lay close to Fort Knox, home of the Armored Forces Command, which was certainly favorable for a future armor camp. The Tennessee Central Railroad, U.S. 41W and Outlaw Air Field represented essential transportation links for the building and sustaining of an Army city-camp, especially for the bringing in of pine board from Georgia to build the all-wooden city-camp. A climate favorable to year-round training and the availability of recreation facilities in nearby Clarksville and Hopkinsville were cited for very favorable consideration. A key technical consideration for selecting the Hopkinsville-Clarksville area was the availability of labor needed to build the camp. The overall strategy of the camp construction program relied on speedy construction to match the rapid personnel expansion. The issue was so important that the War Department dispatched Major A.J. Mitchell specifically to survey the local labor situation in July just prior to the site selection decision in Washington, D.C. It was believed by the writers at the *Kentucky New Era* that the loss of the dark-fire tobacco market (a distinctive tobacco grown for smokeless tobacco products, in which the region specialized and whose products had recently been banned for export by the Neutrality Acts, thus collapsing the local market) accounted for the perception of the availability of the required labor.[19]

Credit must be given to the local boosters who attracted the Zone 5 Quartermaster reconnaissance team to the local area. There is much to be said about the positive cooperation that was generated between a local community that wanted a camp in their area and a national government that needed a favorable location for a camp. It must be remembered that at the time the site selection for the additional twenty-one city-camps was being contemplated, national enthusiasm for incremental mobilization was facing a backlash. Not every location was suitable for a camp, and not every suitable location had a citizenry willing to accept a camp. Imagine, for example, if the Army had tried to build a training center near the University of California at Berkeley campus at the height of the Vietnam War in 1968. The political atmosphere in many locations throughout the United States in July 1942 was similar.

Politics was an important consideration in site selection. Powerful senators like Alban Barkly of Kentucky, the Senate majority leader, and Kenneth McKellar of Tennessee, along with active representatives like J. Percy Priest (TN) and Noble T. Gregory (KY), lobbied heavily on behalf of their constituents and their interest in attracting a camp. Their efforts were appropriate and in keeping with our political tradition. The men who made the site selection decision, men like Brigadier General Brehon Somervell, General George C. Marshall and Secretary of War Henry Stimson, were not the kind of men swayed by mere crass political considerations. But politics were nonetheless a factor. An appreciation for the balance of the Army's analytical criteria and for the local political support required to accept one of these city-camps required mature judgment. Such judgment could be summed up as was described of Brigadier General Somervell: "Although Somervell was committed to building only in a location favorable to military training and expeditious construction, he did not object to choosing a site that also enjoyed political support, Hence, lobbying by state officials and legislators also helped secure the designation of Camp McCoy [a sister site selectee to the Tennessee-Kentucky Armor Camp] as an 'advance planning project.'"[20]

ENGINEERING SURVEY AND LAND APPRAISAL

When Secretary of War Henry Stimson made his final selections on 16 July 1942, Brigadier General Somervell and his Quartermaster Construction Division staff were ready with a list of experienced architect-engineering firms endorsed for carrying out land survey tasks of city-camp magnitude. The commander of Zone 5, Lieutenant Colonel B.F. Vandervoort, contracted with the Lexington-based firm of Wilson, Bell & Watkins. The survey was to be a preliminary one in order to be ready to make the purchase and start construction if an expansion were authorized by Congress. Funding for the preliminary survey work was referred to as Title 1 funding. The funding not yet authorized for land acquisition and construction would be referred to as Title 2 funding, if that eventuality were to occur. The Title 1 survey included all required topographical fieldwork to site the exact location of the boundaries of the camp, preparation of maps for further survey work and a tentative layout of the cantonment. Supporting tasks included survey for rail spurs, water supply and distribution, sewage disposal, roadways and electrical supply system. The survey was estimated to require three and a half months, estimated to be finished by 15 November 1941. It was estimated that labor to support the technical team would provide employment for 250 local people to work as stenographers, linemen, secretaries, rod men and other relatively low-skill-level jobs. Every effort was to be made to employ local people.[21]

Wilson, Bell & Watkins sent an advance team to Clarksville, Tennessee, headed by Stewart Watkins. James K. Latham of the firm was the principal architect, and H. St. Carmichael, recently hired by the firm from a position as the director of the Public Works Administration for Kentucky, was the chief engineer. The advance team chose Clarksville for its headquarters because of its proximity to the field site. Zone 5 also established a field office in Clarksville to oversee the work. The City of Clarksville helped arrange for office space by converting the old Darnell and Bellamy Tobacco Warehouse on North Second Street. The fieldwork began on 30 July 1941. Professor D.V. Terrell, surveying engineer, began the survey in a cornfield at

The principals of the firm of Wilson, Bell & Watkins who designed and built Camp Campbell. *Left to right*: James K. Latham, Grant S. Bell, John F. Wilson, H. St. G. Carmichael and J. Stevens Watkins.

The first day of the survey beginning at the intersection of U.S. 41 West and Kentucky Highway 117. (Highway 117 was then what is now the Gate 6 access road, Morgan Road.)

the corner of what is now U.S. 41A and the Gate 6 Road, Morgan Road. Morgan Road was then Kentucky Highway 117. It was relocated to the north to route civilian traffic north of what was to become Campbell Army

Airfield. The survey first established the future site of the cantonment, then the perimeter of the training area and last the easement that would bring water for the city-camp from the Red River at the southeast corner of the reservation. In late August, Major A.L. Tynes of the surgeon general's office in Washington, D.C., made an inspection of the survey area, and plans were made to include a 1,245-bed Station Hospital site within the cantonment area survey.[22]

The beginning of the survey signaled, perhaps for the first time to many, that the camp was not an abstract but a very real possibility. Three groups of citizens reacted to the realization. First, the Hopkinsville boosters were somewhat taken aback that their project seemed to gravitate out of their orbit to Clarksville, where the presence of Wilson, Bell & Watkins was beginning to make a significant and positive economic impact of the sort they had envisioned for themselves a year earlier. Hopkinsville boosters redoubled their efforts to attract the Army to the federal game reserve area and brought their concern to the attentions of their senators, Alban Barkley and A.B. Chandler. Their efforts were too little, too late, and by that time in the swirl of planning, their efforts came to no avail, but there has been since then a certain coolness that lingers even to this date among some citizens of Hopkinsville toward the camp and the perceived injustice of the benefits accrued by an "undeserving Clarksville."[23] The second group of citizens caught by the reality of the survey was those in Clarksville. Just the influx of persons working in the technical staff of Wilson, Bell & Watkins was enough to impact office space, temporary lodgings and local restaurants. Serious planning began to take place in Clarksville between the mayor and city council about how new federal laws were being designed to help fund infrastructure improvement and expansion projects in communities absorbing the impact of large federal projects. Clarksville mayor William Kleenman applied for over $150 million in grants from the Community Facilities Fund of the PWA for schools, teachers, street repair, sewage improvements and housing construction for 1942 projects.[24] The final group of citizens impacted by the reality of the survey was the local farmers, the rural families who were living on the land that someone was now planning to take from them. That someone was, of course, the government, but the face of the government was that of the survey crews that were now treading across their lands. A great part of their anxiety was driven by uncertainty about where the boundaries might be and if and when they would be forced to move and to where. Rural families in the Tennessee and Kentucky of 1941 were much more isolated then than now. Their information came from

Work progressing on the survey at the temporary headquarters of Wilson, Bell & Watkins at the old Darnell and Bellamy Tobacco Warehouse in Clarksville, Tennessee.

the local paper and the local radio station. Rural families suspected, perhaps rightly so, that the owners and operators of the local press tended to be on the urban side of the divide and under suspicion as potential beneficiaries of the change that would be coming if a giant city-camp were to be built.

Concurrent with the technical work of the land survey was the financial work of the land appraisal. Whereas the purpose of the land survey was to determine boundaries and construction costs, the purpose of the land acquisition survey was to determine the cost of purchasing the land from its owners. The two estimates together would give Washington a reasonable estimate of the cost to build—an estimate of nearly $30 million for construction. The land was fertile and rich and known as the "Black Patch" for the quality dark-fired tobacco raised there. Attempts by agricultural interests to nudge the Army more to the east into Montgomery County, Tennessee, based on the quality of the land were not successful.

The commander of Zone 5 assigned Major John Retter as the land acquisition officer for the project. Mr. M.J. O'Bryan, the Zone 5 real estate director, was assigned as his assistant. Zone 5 contracted with the

Federal Land Bank of Louisville, Kentucky, a private bank experienced in agricultural appraisal, to conduct the survey. Mr. E.E. Shore headed the survey team of eight to ten field appraisers.[25]

There were three types of farmers who owned or who lived on the land: owners, tenants of absentee owners and sharecroppers. There were six small villages that provided basic market and post office services to the local area. Each was affected differently by the appraisal survey. Most farmers in the survey area were those who owned and lived on their own farms. Many owners lived on farms that had long been in their families' possession. For them, the emotional attachment was deep and the resentment caused by survey and appraisal was profound. Among this type of owner was a successful community of black farm owners located around the Woodlawn community in the southeast corner of the survey area in Montgomery County, Tennessee. In the days of Jim Crow segregation in the South, their success was exemplary. The eventual breaking of their community to make way for the city-camp, however, was one of many minor tragedies. The community was not able to relocate and reestablish what it once had.[26]

The second type of owners was the absentee owners. These owners rented their farms to tenant farmers while they themselves lived elsewhere, usually in town (Clarksville). For some of these owners, there was an impending sense of loss but not an impending loss of lifestyle or income. Many reaped a fair profit on a farm that might otherwise not be easy to sell, and they could still count on good fortune in town as civic expansion

A typical rural family near Parker Town displaced by Camp Campbell.

began to bear fruit. For some of these owners, the prospect of the city-camp was a double good fortune. The tenant farmers would be forced to relocate, a great inconvenience to be sure, but federal relocation help would be provided, and there was the prospect of immediate work on the city-camp construction crews to ease the financial burden.

The last group of those depending on the land was sharecroppers and agricultural day laborers, who were almost exclusively black. The Federal Farm Services Administration (FSA) assisted sharecroppers and day laborers to find work elsewhere, not unlike an employment agency.

The rules for the appraisal were simple and based on experience with the camp construction program. Schemes to profit from the process by real estate and land speculators were obstructed. Major Retter explained and enforced that the government would deal only with the properly titled property owners as of the August 4 date of the beginning of the appraisal. To this end, an attorney from each county (Montgomery and Stuart in Tennessee and Trigg and Christian in Kentucky) was hired to do a title search and resolve all property title issues in preparation for a possible land acquisition. Appraisals were conducted face to face, farm to farm, field to field. Buildings, fences and crops were included. A separate appraisal team conducted a timber survey. Timber that could be harvested for construction was added to farm appraisals as appropriate. The progress of the appraisal followed the same path as the survey: cantonment area, water easement and maneuver/range areas. The appraisal was not finished until 5 January 1942, almost one month after the Pearl Harbor attack that resulted in the end of incremental mobilization and only one day prior to congressional authorization for Title 2 funding for immediate construction of the city-camp. The actual cost of the property buyout was just over $4 million, but it seems that the cost established by the appraisal was not a significant factor, if at all, in the final set of criteria for determination to build the city-camp.

From the beginning of the survey through the 6 January 1942 announcement to fund construction, there was a lingering doubt about whether the city-camp would become a reality. For some, farmers in particular, the doubt gave rise to the hope that perhaps it was all much ado about nothing, that the excitement would pass. Every newspaper article about the progress of the survey and appraisal seemed to end with a reminder that, despite this activity or the other, no decision about the city-camp had been made. In those months before Pearl Harbor, the hope that the crucible of war might pass loomed large in the national discussion. That

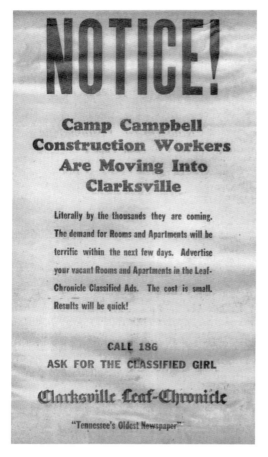

NOTICE!

Camp Campbell Construction Workers Are Moving Into Clarksville

Literally by the thousands they are coming. The demand for Rooms and Apartments will be terrific within the next few days. Advertise your vacant Rooms and Apartments in the Leaf-Chronicle Classified Ads. The cost is small. Results will be quick!

**CALL 186
ASK FOR THE CLASSIFIED GIRL**

Clarksville Leaf-Chronicle

"Tennessee's Oldest Newspaper"

Finding temporary housing for the ten thousand men who responded to the need for construction workers taxed local resources. A call to the three-digit number for the "Classified Girl" at the *Clarksville Leaf-Chronicle* allowed locals to offer extra rooms for rent.

Congress continued to restrain from further funding for incremental mobilization indicated a political caution because of the neutrality mood. For powerful men like Roosevelt, Stimson and Marshall and powerful politicians in Washington like Alban Barkley, there was the inside knowledge of knowing not if, but when, international events would tip the country into war.

As 1941 came to a close, farmers fretted about what plans to make to make for the coming season: to plant, to husband livestock? City fathers fretted about the potential to overwhelm the local black and white school districts if there were a population surge and how to expand the infrastructure to accommodate change. The best advice offered was to plan as if there were to be no city-camp, plan as if there were to be no war. Waiting was all they could do while an uncomfortable anxiety hung over their world.

CHAPTER 3

LAND ACQUISITION AND CONSTRUCTION

Pearl Harbor ended incremental mobilization and the American Neutrality Movement. Large three-inch font—a font size reserved for only the most momentous of news—announced the attack and the declaration of war on the masthead of the *Clarksville Leaf-Chronicle*. M-Day had arrived. Twenty-nine days later, on 6 January 1942, speculation about the Tennessee-Kentucky Armor Camp was settled. In that same three-inch font read on the *Clarksville Leaf-Chronicle* "Camp Authorized." The headline indicated that the news of the day was as momentous as had been the attack on Pearl Harbor.

The transition from appraisal and survey to acquisition and construction was nearly seamless. Major John Retter was the land appraisal officer when he went to bed on 5 January and woke up as the land acquisition officer on the sixth. Wilson, Bell & Watkins was immediately awarded the contract to manage Title 2 construction for the project. Its engineer survey was not even cold on the shelf and the firm had not yet even finished closing down its Clarksville operations when the new contract was offered. It was a tremendous boon for the project that those who knew it so intimately in its conception were there to start the acquisition and construction, missing hardly a beat. The circumstances provided an exceptional head start on construction and perfectly validated the wisdom of General Marshall's advance planning initiative of May 1941. The only change to the management team was the result of a Truman Committee recommendation that future camp and major construction be consolidated under the Army

Corps of Engineers. The consolidation of the Quartermaster Construction Division and the Army Corps of Engineers Construction Division had been carefully managed in Washington, D.C., between the two agencies. Personnel were transferred between the divisions to ensure continuity. As construction began at the city-camp, Army oversight was transferred from Quartermaster Zone 5, Columbus, Ohio, to U.S. Army Corps of Engineers, Nashville District. Captain Kenneth Wysong of the Corps Nashville District Office was assigned to oversee the construction.

LAND ACQUISITION

Mr. L.B. Harington of Madisonville, Kentucky, headed a team of eight government negotiators who handled the mechanics of the land acquisition. Their process was quick, efficient and very nearly ruthless. They had to be quick about their work. Construction was due to begin immediately in the cantonment area. They had until 10 February to settle and evacuate the properties therein. The water easement was next in the priority of their work. The remainder of the maneuver and range area could be finished by June. The negotiators allowed the property owners to offer a price. If the price offered was within the value of the earlier appraisal—a price to which the government negotiators were privy but the owners were not—then the government would conclude a direct sale. If the owner would not offer a price within the appraisal value, the owner could exercise his right to protest the offered price in court.[27] The court proceedings took place at the U.S. District Court for the Middle District of Tennessee in Nashville and resulted in a condemnation hearing, wherein the government would take possession of the land, usually at a slightly higher price than the appraisal price, but take the land nonetheless.[28] There was no escaping that. In the cantonment area, 125 tracts of land (102 in Tennessee and 23 from Kentucky), representing 6,335 acres, were referred by property owners to the District Court.[29] These early numbers reflected a high degree of dissatisfaction with the appraisal. One must remember, too, that travel to Nashville was seen as a place far away and practically foreign to many rural families in those days before the interstate. This in itself was a reflection of the intensity of feeling many people had toward the prospect of losing their land.

Landowners and farmers had concerns beyond just the appraised value of their property. First, there was the cost and inconvenience of moving a farm operation. Those expenses had not been calculated into raw property value. Second, the timeline for evacuation of the property was ten to twenty days, especially in the cantonment area. Even though the acquisition had been rumored for months, most families had not taken preliminary and necessary relocation steps. Finally, the appraisal value was calculated at a peacetime value and the new property to which owners would relocate would be purchased at a higher wartime value. There was unfairness about having to sell land at low peacetime economy prices and then be forced to buy at high wartime economy prices, on average up to ten dollars per acre more.

Working against time, a number of farmers and landowners organized and hired two attorneys, H.B Stout and A.B. Broadbent, of Clarksville, on 27 January. Two local landowners and the two attorneys departed for Washington, D.C., four days later. They met first with their senators and representatives at the Capitol for encouragement and then headed to the War Department to plead their case. They were seeking a 10 to 50 percent increase in the appraisal valuation. As a result of their efforts, the War Department sent Mr. George E. Miller of the Real Estate Division to Clarksville to investigate the complaints. Mr. Miller arrived on 4 February, conducted a three-day investigation and returned to Washington on the seventh. His findings and report were expected to be published in the *Leaf-Chronicle* on 9 February. Mr. Miller's report, however, was not made public by the War Department. Nothing was published; nothing was ever heard again about the report. Having given it their best effort, many landowners resigned themselves to their fate. The acquisition team continued its grim work quickly, efficiently and nearly ruthlessly until completion in late June 1942. The acquisition work was followed by federal marshals who served and enforced eviction notices. Nearly one-third of owners continued the one form of resistance left to them: the condemnation hearings. In the end, 1,105 tracts of land representing 101,755.44 acres were obtained by the government. Of these, 756 tracts of land (67,758 acres) were sold by direct sale and 376 tracts of land (33,831 acres) were obtained by condemnation hearing. Those figures reveal that almost half the rural property owners went to court rather than accept the 1941 government land appraisal values.[30] To underscore the point, as of 2012, seventy years later, several cases still linger as contested in the U.S. District Court.

Relocation, Crops, Bodies, Buildings and Roads

Taking ownership of the land was not the end of the land acquisition story. In fairness, the government and the local counties did provide significant relocation services. The FSA opened a relocation office in Clarksville and sought to match relocating families with available farms in adjoining counties. The office offered services through the end of May 1942. The FSA also sought to match sharecroppers and agricultural workers with employment opportunities. As a means of financial compensation in an attempt to redress some of the concerns resulting from the austerity of the 1941 property appraisal methodology, a crop buy-back program and crop allotment adjustments program provided extra income to help defray the costs of the moving and relocation of operations of farm families. Farmers who had crops on their land, the value of which had been assessed and for which they had received initial compensation, were allowed to buy back hay and crops at a discounted price and transfer them to their new farms. Crops for which there had been a federal allotment, tobacco in particular, were adjusted so that farmers would retain the right to sell the amount of commodity authorized from the condemned farm, as well as that for the new farm allotment. This one-year program took some of the sting out of relocation expenses. In addition to these government efforts, Lawrence County, Tennessee, provided a bus and tour for local farmers in an attempt to welcome them and attract them to available properties for sale in their county.[31]

A secondary issue that required resolution was the reinterment of the dead. In March 1942, the government accepted the responsibility to cover the cost of reinterment. In those bygone days when racial segregation applied even to bodies, a reinternment site on the property of Viola Farley near La Fayette, Kentucky, was established for "white bodies," and a site on the property of W.P. Hambaugh on the Britton Church Road north of the west end of the maneuver area was selected for "colored bodies." Some long-standing resident families took advantage of the government offer. Some did not because they believed that after the war, if the city-camp were to be disestablished, they would be returning to their homes and to the graves of their loved ones. For some new arrival families, however, the small cemetery plots on their land belonged to previous owners who had long departed the area. Having no family connection, they moved and left the plots as they were. The result of the program was that 179 grave sites were not moved.

The government agreed to take responsibility for the care and maintenance of the sites—and continues to do so to this date through the office of the Director of Public Works (DPW) at Fort Campbell.[32]

Across the 102,000 acres the government acquired stood hundreds of buildings: homes, barns, sheds, stores, schools, churches…The vast majority were sold at government auction for salvage. A few were put to use in the making of a mock German village in the training area called Hitlerville. Several homes near the access roads on the north and west end of the maneuver/range area lasted into the late 1960s. They were used as housing for a few selected NCOs who served as game wardens. Those buildings, too, are now gone. Though there is precious little in the way of ruins, one can still discern some of the old home locations while traversing the maneuver/range area. A copse of trees, volunteer daffodils in the spring and an occasional tangle of wild rose reveal a homestead location; perhaps it is even in the vicinity of a small fenced cemetery that provides an additional clue. The concrete foundation of the Parker Town store can still be seen near the base of the range tower of Range 42 just off the Jordon Springs Road.

Four buildings are all that remain of the pre-camp era. One of those buildings, the Childers House, is in the maneuver/range area. It was built in 1938–39 by James Childers. It is a beautiful brick building patterned after Gunston Hall, the home of Founding Father George Mason in Northern Virginia. The building is located on the Mabry Road in the vicinity of Cassidy Range (DF 542532). It was used for a time as housing for senior NCOs and

One of six small communities displaced by Camp Campbell, Parker Town. The remains of the store foundation can still be seen behind the range tower on Range 46.

later as a facility for Special Forces interrogation training; a two-way mirror was installed in the living room for that purpose. Most recently, it has been used as the office of the Cultural Recourses Division of the Department of Public Works. At present, the building falls into the range safety exclusion zone for Cassidy Range. It has been vacated pending further disposition.

Two of the remaining four buildings are located in Cole Park, the senior officer housing area at Fort Campbell. These two beautiful buildings have been preserved and restored and have been in service as senior officer housing since the 1950s. The first home is called the Log Cabin, although it is anything but a cabin. It was built in 1932 by Winfield Durrett. It was built of chestnut logs, white oak interior finishes and red oak flooring. For many years, it served as the quarters of choice for the commanding general or, if not the commanding general, then one of the assistant division commanders. The second building is called the Cole House, though it has no relation to Medal of Honor recipient Lieutenant Colonel Robert Cole, for whom the housing area is named. The Cole House was built in the 1930s and went

The Log Cabin located in the Cole Park Housing Area. It is one of four buildings surviving from the preconstruction era. The log cabin has served as home to the commanding general from time to time when that individual preferred it to Aspen Plains. It will likely be brought down in 2015.

Quarters 1544

A sketch of the Cole House, a preconstruction building located in Cole Park. The house is named for the last owner of the house before it was appropriated for the camp, Dr. Cole. The housing area called Cole Park is named in honor of Lieutenant Colonel Robert Cole, first Medal of Honor winner in the 101st Airborne Division.

through a number of owners up to H.R. Cole, who owned it last before the acquisition. It is a one-and-a-half-story brick home. The building has served as family housing for general officers and as a community center building within Cole Park.

The fourth surviving building is the only pre–Civil War building on the installation. It was called the General's Quarters or Quarters 101. The building is just to the right as one enters the installation through Gate 4. The original part of the house, built as a log cabin in 1833, has been incorporated into a larger, two-story frame house. In the 1870s, it became known in the local area by the name Aspin Plantation, a four-hundred-acre farm complete with a horse-racing track that was located on the south side of Gate 4 in what is now the Mahaffey Middle School soccer field. Jefferson Davis, former president of the Confederate States, spent a night here as a guest while touring the area in 1870. Davis was born in nearby Fairview, Kentucky. The building was used as the post guardhouse during World War II for the Gate 4 guard detail. It began to be used as quarters for general officers in the early 1950s and alternated with the log cabin as the official quarters of the commanding general for a number of years. It was recognized as the official general officer quarters of the commanding general until 2014, when new quarters for the commanding general were

Aspen Plains often served as the home of the commanding general.

built. Aspen Plains, however, will continue to serve the city as a building for use by family support activities.

A total of 100 to 150 miles of roads connected the small communities and farms now incorporated into the maneuver/range area, "the back 40," as it came to be called by the soldiers. As in any rural area, the roads varied between hard surface impervious roads and dirt/dry weather roads. The better-quality impervious surface roads ran east–west and greatly facilitated moving soldiers and combat vehicles to the training ranges. Most of the roads retained their pre-camp names. Mabry Road and Jordon Springs Road, for example, are still primary avenues for moving from the cantonment to the ranges. Where new roads were added in the early days of the camp, they tended to be given functional names such as Artillery Road, West Perimeter Road or Engineer Road. After a time, the new roads in the maneuver area were named in honor of specific units; Angles Road (11th Airborne Division), Ghost Corps Trail (XX Armor Corps) and Destiny Trail (101st Airborne Division) are examples. As the roads throughout the area were improved, small bridges were added over creeks to improve mobility, and each bridge seemed to be memorialized in honor of a soldier who had earned a medal for heroism. No plaques were attached to those bridges, and the soldier for whom a bridge was memorialized is a matter of historical record in a file cabinet. The current protocol for the naming of any new road that might be added to the maneuver area is to seek a name reminiscent of the pre-camp era rather than using a name of an individual or an incident from unit history, as is the practice in the cantonment area. Pot Neck Road in the northwest of the maneuver area was named as a result of a suggestion that the term "pot neck" was used as slang for "one who was not mentally quick" in the area of the small town of Bumpus Mills years and years ago. Brodie Brothers Road in the northeast recalls a pair of colorful, eccentric and very wealthy brothers who owned a farm on the border of the installation in the 1940s.

CONSTRUCTION

Construction was the process by which the concept for the city-camp became a reality. In the nine months between January 1942, when the first bids went out, and September, when the completed project was accepted by the Army, over twenty-six million square feet of barracks, warehouses, maintenance

Construction of troop billets along Tennessee Avenue by subcontractor Whittenberg Construction Company.

facilities, etc., were constructed. An electrical grid, a water distribution and sewage system, miles of hard surface roads within the city-camp and miles of railroad track to support the construction and future military operations were laid. Roads, ranges, bivouac areas and maneuver training areas to support the training of the Army's most modern armor divisions were built and in place and ready to begin training by June. The scope and magnitude of the project was huge: the successful completion in a mere nine months was an engineering phenomenon but a phenomenon that was the product of the accumulated experience of building sixty-one camps in the period of incremental mobilization.

Because of the firm's excellent work on the Title 1 survey, it was not surprising that Wilson, Bell & Watkins was awarded the contract to supervise the Title 2 construction project. At times up to fifteen subcontractors were under their supervision. H. St. George Carmichel was retained as the chief engineer on the project, and James K. Latham continued to serve as the principal architect. The Clarksville Chamber of Commerce arranged for a temporary construction headquarters facility in the W.H. Simmons warehouse on Front Street in Clarksville. The company headquarters moved from Clarksville to the camp construction site in April.

GETTING STARTED

Carmichel and Latham had two tasks that needed to occur nearly simultaneously to get the project going. The first step for the company was to lay out the street grid for the cantonment. The second was to advertise and begin the bid process for subcontractor labor. The subcontract process for construction labor did not go well at first. Most of those bids were rejected as overpriced or underqualified. The bid process had to be altered slightly by the Corps of Engineers from an advertised bid system to a negotiated bid system. The change of system worked, and contracts began to be signed. While the street grid design project was underway, two important early bids were accepted and work began. An early bid for the grading of the cantonment area and the rail spur was accepted from the Forcum-James Company of Dyersburg, Tennessee. Its first project, and the first recorded project in the building of the camp, was to build the berm supporting a trestle bridge on the east side of Highway 41W (Fort Campbell Boulevard) that would connect the future camp rail spur to the existing Tennessee

Central Railroad line. Although the original trestle bridge has been replaced, the current bridge is in the same location spanning the now four-lane Fort Campbell Boulevard in the vicinity of Gate 2. It serves as a reminder of the importance of rail connectivity as a site selection criterion in 1941, as well as a reminder of how critical rail connectivity remains today as a major means of deployment for the modern units at Fort Campbell. Forcum-James then began the work of grading the cantonment area. Second in priority to grading the cantonment area was the installation of the water and sewage system. It was essential for the underground water, sewage and storm drain pipe system to be laid before construction of the buildings could begin. This contract was awarded to the E.H. Marhauffer Company of Chicago. Harsh winter weather that slowed projects all across the United States in 1942 and a labor dispute hampered the grading and water system work in February. The labor issue will be explained further in a later section.

THE STREET GRID

The design for the street grid of the cantonment in 1942 had a very simple logic. Despite subsequent construction since 1945, and even in spite of a few street name changes since then, the logic of the original design is still very much discernible today. The modern city traffic flow continues to be influenced by the original design. For ease of naming, the avenues running south to north were named for the forty-eight states. The streets running east to west were numbered starting from 1st Street in the south and ending with 59th Street in the north. The very center of the street grid, and located on the highest elevation in the cantonment area, was the center point of the grid, between 25th and 26th Streets. The center of the street grid is where T-39, the division headquarters building, was placed. The center of the street grid also divided the cantonment half in Tennessee (1st to 25th Street) and half in Kentucky (26th to 59th Street). Missouri, Tennessee, Kentucky and Indiana Avenues ran the length of the cantonment south to north and formed the core, or the spine, of the street grid.

Six access roads into the camp were built on the east side of the cantonment from Highway 41W. They were numbered from south to north as Gate 1 in the south to Gate 6 in the north. The main gate access was Gate 4, which led to the center of the city-camp. The Gate 4 access road was named in honor of the first commander of the Armored Forces

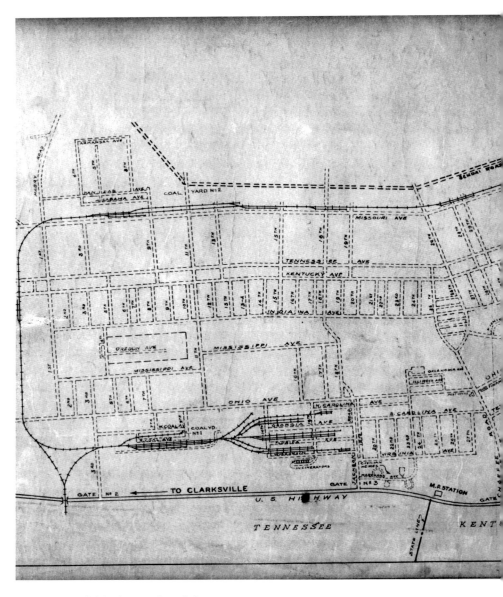

A map of the finished street plan of the cantonment area.

Command, Major General Adna Chaffee, who had recently passed away. From south to north, the access street at Gate 1 was named for Robert E. Lee; the Gate 2 access street remained simply 3rd Street; the Gate 3 access street was named in honor of Tennessean and President Andrew

Jackson; the Gate 5 access street was named for Confederate cavalry officer Nathan Bedford Forrest; and the Gate 6 access street (the former Kentucky Highway 117) was renamed for Confederate cavalry officer John Hunt Moran. The streets in the Station Hospital area were named in honor of heroes of the Army Medical Corps: Drs. Walter Reed, Jonathon Letterman and William Gorgas.

The spine of the cantonment area, defined by the area between Kentucky and Indiana Avenues, was that area where the unit troop barracks were laid out and organized unit by unit in line to compose all the subordinate units of an armor division. All the buildings in the spine were oriented north–south. The Division Headquarters, Building T-39, and the "city center" of the camp lay in the middle of that street grid between 25th and 26th Streets. The core, or spine, the north–south avenues, made a slight twenty-degree angle to the left at the center point (between 25th and 26th Streets) in keeping with curvilinear design.

It is a feature of the curvilinear design that in the middle of the grid Chaffee Road split left and right in front of T-39, forming a Y shape in the street pattern. The right side, 26th Street, was one-way traffic west for several blocks to Tennessee Avenue. If one were to turn left (south) on Tennessee Avenue, travel one block to 25th Street and turn left, traffic was one-way east back toward Chaffee Road. Within this Y in the center of the street grid was built the Division Headquarters (T-39). Behind T-39 were a guest house for visitors, a service club and the post athletic field house. These four buildings provided unique service for the whole camp, and all four buildings were oriented to face Gate 4, thereby highlighting in the Y a visible "city center." Subsequently in the 1950s and 1960s, construction of the city center theme would continue to include buildings and facilities that served post-wide recreation and entertainment purposes. New buildings were added on the outside or perimeter of the Y. Some of the latter construction included, for example, Wilson Theater (1950s), the 1970s PX and the Sink Library. Near the Y, the post athletic field and stadium (Fryar Field) and the post baseball field (Perez Field, no longer used) were placed, highlighting the center of the cantonment as the city center.

The motor pools and maintenance facilities for the divisional units were lined up south to north on the west side of Tennessee Avenue parallel to the unit barracks. By such a design, the troops in training lived adjacent to their motor pools. Each unit motor pool had a hard stand surface, enclosed maintenance buildings and an outdoor grease rack. The motor pools were arranged south to north to allow for direct and easy access to Range Road and, from Range Road, easy access west into the training area road network system.

Troop housing for the units of the Garrison Command (1580th Service Command) were located between Indiana and Ohio Avenues and also between South Carolina and Virginia Avenues. The industrial area where the warehouses, the post facility engineer and third echelon maintenance facilities were located was east of Ohio Avenue. The "industrial corner" of

T-39 in the center of the Y formed by 25th and 26th Streets.

the cantonment was supported by rail spurs and sidings that allowed rail cars to pull up next to the warehouse buildings for easy loading and unloading by forklift through large rolling doors on the sides of the buildings. The post laundry was located in the industrial corner at the corner of Jackson Street and Ohio Avenue (now Bastogne and Air Assault).

All of the Army's World War II city-camps were administered by a garrison command unit. At Camp Campbell, this unit was the 1580th Service Command Unit. The garrison commander, a colonel, had his own headquarters building separate from T-39. Not surprisingly, the garrison headquarters building was named T-1. This World War II arrangement allowed the commanders of the units in training to be free of all administrative and logistical responsibility for running the camp. This allowed them to concentrate on the training and deploying of their units.

The camp headquarters area at the intersection of what is now Bastogne and Screaming Eagle Boulevard. The Planters Bank and Trust Building runs parallel to Bastogne (Ohio). The building in the foreground is T-1, camp commander's headquarters. These buildings were on the site of what is now is the George Turner Guest House.

The original post office located on the corner of Chaffee (Screaming Eagle Boulevard) and Ohio (Bastogne). When approaching the intersection from Gate 4, the post office was located on the left, or southwest, corner, on the side where the education center is now located.

The garrison headquarters and staff provided for all administration of the camp and training facilities. T-1 was located inside the main entrance, Gate 4, within a headquarters complex of six buildings at the intersection of Ohio and Chaffee Avenues (now Bastogne and Screaming Eagle Boulevard).

The garrison command headquarters was at an intersection two blocks inside Gate 4. It was two blocks before the Y split in Chaffee Road. Visitors entering the camp through Gate 4 drove two blocks inside the camp and arrived first at the garrison headquarters complex and then, if continuing west several more blocks, at the city center and headquarters of the major unit in training at building T-39. A commercial bank, Planters Bank (T-15) and the U.S. Post Office (T-4) were located at the intersection in the near vicinity of the garrison headquarters. Interestingly, Gate 4, the post office (T-4) and the garrison command headquarters (T-1) were just barely on the Kentucky side of the state line, whereas the division headquarters (T-39) was on the Tennessee side of the state line.

LABOR, SUBCONTRACTING AND FINISHING THE PROJECT

As the street grid design and the initial grading began in the midst of harsh and disagreeable February weather, a newly invigorated labor movement interjected itself on the camp construction program. The Wagner Act of 1935, a centerpiece of the president's Second New Deal program, had a shaky start and didn't gain full acceptance until it survived a Supreme Court challenge, after which the new law gave encouragement to the labor movement to pursue the provisions of the act. The act had established the National Labor Relations Board (NLRB), an independent agency with powers to oversee the appropriate bargaining units representing labor. By 1942, many labor organizations were making use of their reinvigorated status and encouragement of the federal government to press their claims, especially where federal dollars were being spent on the camp construction program. For example, Forcum-James of Nashville, which had won the contract for grading Camp Campbell, did not hire union labor for the project. The Nashville Building Trade Council challenged the practice. Rather than going to court and assuredly interrupting the camp project progress, however, the Department of Labor dispatched a negotiator, Mr. G.C. Peek, to Clarksville. A mediation meeting was held on 4–5 March at the Hotel Montgomery in downtown Clarksville. The arbitration resulted in a compromise that the construction project would indeed be a union shop project but not a closed shop project. The agreement provided that priority of hiring would go first to the Nashville Building Trade Council, and then it allowed subcontractors to hire non-union labor once union labor was exhausted. Hired non-union labor, however, would be required in time to join the union. The compromise satisfied the union by effectively mandating the use of union labor, and it satisfied the subcontractors who were involved in relatively short-term projects and were most concerned to hire necessary labor immediately, union or not, to get on with the job.

The winter storms and labor disputes of February gave way to milder weather and labor reconciliation in March. The grading and water projects were well underway. The success of the new negotiated bid system paved the way for rapid progress. The bids of three major construction subcontractors were accepted: Niles Yearwood of Nashville, Whitenbourg Construction of Louisville and O'Driscoll & Grove Company of Chicago. Buildings arose, and progress never slowed, not for lack of labor, material or construction management techniques. Even as early as the end of March, just within the first weeks of the project, it was reported that construction crews were erecting buildings at the pace of a mere matter of days per unit. The pace quickened within a month to individual crews putting up several buildings per day as new prefabrication techniques were perfected. By September, only seven months later, the city-camp was ready for occupation by twenty-three thousand soldiers.

The almost frantic pace of construction was not unique to Camp Campbell. The pace was by design. First and foremost, the standardized design of the 700 and 800 Series plan and the simple construction diagrams were easily adaptable to unskilled labor, and most of the construction labor employed by the War Department for the camp construction program was unskilled. Camp construction was temporary work, and skilled carpentry labor tended to gravitate to the WPA jobs that provided the security of permanent employment. It was estimated that the labor force working on the camp construction program grew from 5,380 in June 1940 when the program began to 396,255 by the time construction began at Camp Campbell. Up to 10,000 workers were involved in the Camp Campbell project.

Innovative construction management and techniques played a large role in the construction pace. Assembly-line techniques such as dividing workers into teams trained to do discrete portions of the task—framing a wall, for example—allowed the workers to move from building to building, each team

The makeshift field construction office of the building subcontractor O'Driscoll & Grove.

doing its part. Prefabrication at central sawmills of sections such as roofs, trusses, joists and bracing, etc., was a new technique, as was the idea of moving a series of saws from block to block in order to have a saw crew cut standardized parts on demand for the assembly crews. These innovations perfected in the camp construction program would profoundly affect the building industry after the war, when the need for plenty and affordable housing led to the development of massive suburban subdivisions. The techniques born of wartime construction became standard throughout the construction industry in the booming 1950s.

While the cantonment area was nearing completion, construction of the ranges and maneuver area intensified. Residents were given until June and July to clear from the farther out maneuver and range areas. The ghost town remains of the six small villages and hundreds of farms slowly, but not completely at first, came down.[33] The specifications for tank, artillery and infantry qualification ranges were spelled out in Army training manuals. The training program was designed to take a bunch of raw recruits and transform them into a combat-ready division. It was called the MTP, or

Mobilization Training Program. The MTP for armored divisions required nine months of rigorous training to make the transformation.

Near the cantonment, easily within walking distance of the troop billets, were the small arms ranges. Squad maneuver and infiltration ranges were added on the north and west perimeter of this small arms impact area. Mortar, artillery and heavy caliber weapons ranges were established around a north and a south impact area at the west end of the reservation. To these impact areas were added sophisticated maneuver ranges for combined arms gunnery and maneuver. A range in the north impact area was developed for air support air-to-ground gunnery. A combat range named Hitlerville that simulated a German village was located in the center of the maneuver area (near the location of present-day Craig Village: DL 465535). Hitlerville exposed soldiers to the harsh realities of street fighting and in many ways was a rustic ancestor of the modern Cassidy Village used for the same purpose today. The southern half of the maneuver area was dedicated to non-gunnery training and bivouac areas. The range layout established in 1942 continued to develop throughout the war as units devised more complex training scenarios, but the general outline of close-in qualification ranges; an urban combat training facility in the middle; and heavy weapons, aerial gunnery and live-fire maneuver ranges in the western impact areas continues today.

The city-camp and the training ranges were ready for occupation in mid-September 1942. The official activation date for the camp and the activation of the first armored division to occupy it, the 12th Armored Division, were celebrated jointly on 15 September. Construction was not over, however. Additional appropriations for more troop housing were authorized in June and October. Funds for a pool, three POW stockades and additional service clubs were authorized in 1943. The additional troop housing brought the housing availability from the planned 23,000 up to wartime high of housing for 33,011 enlisted men and women and 1,738 officers. In the life of the city, the four years between 1943 and 1947 were the only lag time of any kind in construction funding and activity in an otherwise unbroken history of expansion, upgrade and modernization.

A Name and a Location

The working name of the city-camp in its planning stage, June 1941–January 1942, was the Kentucky-Tennessee Armor Camp. The Army had a long tradition of naming camps and forts in honor of great military or political people. The tradition continued with the naming of World War II camps. In deference to local customs and also to encourage enthusiasm and patronage for the local camps, the War Department solicited recommendations for names from local communities. The solicitation for names for the Tennessee-Kentucky Armor Camp kicked off a lively local debate on both sides of the border.

Favorites on the Tennessee side of the border included Camp Woodrow Wilson, as the parents of the former president had once lived in Clarksville. Clarksville residents also offered the name of Confederate president Jefferson Davis, who was born in nearby Fairview, Kentucky. Austin Peay, a former Tennessee governor; George Rogers Clark, a War for Independence war hero for whom Clarksville was named; and Douglas MacArthur, because the battle for the Philippines had just begun, were all suggested. Representative Noble T. Gregory of Kentucky's First Congressional District pushed for the name of Colonel Henry Burnett, a Kentuckian turned Confederate in the Civil War. Despite the request to solicit names, the War Department had the final say. The War Department chose the name of William Bowen Campbell, a distinguished soldier who had served in the Tennessee Volunteer Regiment as a captain in the Seminole War (1831–33), as the regiment commander of that same regiment in the Mexican-American War (1846–47) and as a brigadier general in the Union for one year in the Civil War (1862–63). Campbell also distinguished himself as a member of the Tennessee state legislature (1838), as a three-time member of the U.S. House of Representatives (1837–42 and 1865–67) and as a governor of Tennessee (1852–54). When the name William Bowen Campbell was announced, it was presumed in the local press that the War Department had selected a neutral name so as not to favor either Clarksville or Hopkinsville. Campbell, a distinguished Southerner who had remained loyal to the Union, seemed an apt compromise that would offend neither the citizenry of Clarksville nor Hopkinsville.

The name Camp Campbell was announced in the local press on 23 February. The official general orders from the War Department, GO 12, 6 March 1942, made the name official: "Camp Campbell, *Clarksville, Tennessee*." The designation of Clarksville, Tennessee, by the War Department in Washington, D.C., was understandable. Two-thirds of the camp (but less than one-half of the cantonment) was located in Tennessee. The survey and early construction headquarters were located in Clarksville. T-39 was located in Tennessee. The post office (T-4) and the 1580th Service Unit Command and Post Headquarters (T-1), however, were located in Kentucky. The post office was so close to the state line, by

Left: Colonel William Bowen Campbell, commander of 1st Tennessee Volunteer Regiment, 1846.

Below: Two cancellation stamps attest to the confusion about the proper location for the camp.

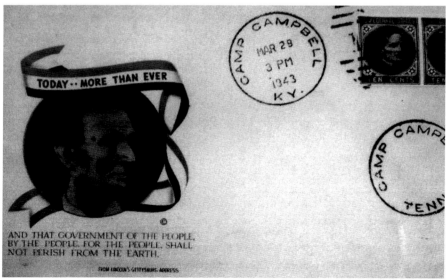

only tens of feet, that the line cut through the parking lot. T-1 was just across the street from the post office, and it, too, straddled the state line by less than a block. There was, it was alleged, a problem for mail delivery because of the confusion. Commercial bus and train schedules were also affected. The historical record is very unclear, but the post commander, Colonel Guy Chipman, was a native of Kentucky, and after three months of confusion, he did petition the War Department to address the problem. Legend suggests that Senator Alban Barkley (D, KY) may have exerted some influence over the War Department from his office as Senate majority leader. The War Department did address Colonel Chipman's concerns and, perhaps with the power of some "Kentucky bias," issued GO 48, 23 September 1942. The order changed the official address from "Camp Campbell, *Clarksville, Tennessee*," to "Camp Campbell, *Kentucky*," without adding Hopkinsville by name.

KEY DATES IN THE CONSTRUCTION OF THE CAMP

6 January 1942: Congress authorizes Title 2 funding for the Tennessee-Kentucky Armored Camp.

2 February 1942: Construction actually begins with the grading of the east berm for the railroad trestle bridge over 41W (U.S. 41A).

6 March 1942: The camp is officially named Camp Campbell, Clarksville, Tennessee.

1 July 1942: A cadre of the 1580th SCU, the first Army unit, is assigned to the camp. This date was considered by the World War II post commanders to be the official activation or "birthday" date of the camp.

15 September 1942: Ceremonial activation of the camp takes place in a joint ceremony with the official activation of the 12th Armored Division.

CHAPTER 4
CAMP CAMPBELL IN WORLD WAR II

THE GIANT BACHELOR CITY

The Army of World War II was built in the giant city-camps like Camp Campbell. Combat divisions and corps headquarters were assembled, organized, equipped, trained and prepared for embarkation in these city-camps. These combat units went on to earn the laurels of victory, and history recorded their deeds. Not so glorious, and seldom remembered, are those who ran and manned the camps that were so integral to the building of the victorious Army.

Managing an Army of eight million men and deploying them around the world was a tremendous endeavor. Organizing, training and deploying divisions from the city-camps seemed simple enough in 1941. As the war effort grew in complexity, more use was demanded of the camps than was originally envisioned. Units needed to be fed into overseas theaters as the commanders needed them, not merely because they had completed their training. Transports needed to be marshaled and built into convoys, supplies for the invasion build-up needed to be moved and priorities often changed. Units were sometimes shuffled from camp to camp based on availability of transportation for deployment into theater, for additional or remedial training needs or even because of restructuring of unit organization as the war progressed.

The Tennessee-Kentucky Armor Camp was conceived and designed in 1941 as a camp at which to train one armored division at a time. The mission grew substantially almost as soon as Camp Campbell was first occupied. From September 1942 to October 1944, one combat division was always in training. Beginning in March 1943, a second division was simultaneously assigned to the camp. It was a training division whose mission was to train all the armored forces individual overseas replacement soldiers. This division, the 20th Armored Division, was fifteen thousand men strong. It trained over thirty thousand replacements. By the end of the war, when replacements were no longer required, it was converted into a combat division. It deployed to Europe and fought in eight days of combat before the war's end. The 20th Armored Division overlapped all the other divisions that trained here (12th AD, 26th ID and 14th AD).

In addition to armored and infantry divisions, two corps headquarters, XX Corps and XXII Corps, trained at Camp Campbell one after the other. From September 1943 to December 1945, there was always a corps headquarters in training overlapping two divisions in training. Corps headquarters varied in number and composition but were made mostly of an assortment of reconnaissance, signal, artillery, tank destroyer and antiaircraft units numbering about three thousand soldiers. In rough numbers, then, there were always at least twenty-eight thousand soldiers in training, plus the camp garrison of over five thousand soldiers. Additionally, to stretch the housing problem just a little further, a Women's Army Corps (WAC) unit was assigned in March 1943 and a prisoner of war camp for three thousand members of the Afrika Korps was established at Camp Campbell from mid-1943 to 1946. Several battalions of various support and engineer troops belonging to the 2nd Army lived at the camp as tenant units. Numerous field hospitals trained here from time to time under the guidance of the staff of the Station Hospital. The numbers of soldiers assigned at the camp always exceeded the original expectation of twenty-three thousand soldiers. Additional construction of some Series 800 buildings in 1943 and the construction of three POW compounds partially made up the difference. The most critical troop housing need was for the soldiers of the 20th AD. Stopgap buildings called hutments—tarpaper-covered plywood shacks—filled the shortfall. With a nonstop schedule and rotation of units through the camp, the wear and tear on the wooden facilities and macadam roads was brutal.

There is no doubt that the training and life of a GI was rigorous. There was, too, a lighter side to camp life. There was a time in the early days of the war, the days before D-Day (June 1944), when there was a bit of the surreal. Everybody in the nation was in motion. The "boys," as they were called, were off to "camp," and in so many ways, it was more like summer camp than Army camp. "It sometimes seemed more like college than the army," observed a member of the 20th AD cadre in the unit's history. The movies of Hollywood at the time, so available in the Army theaters at each camp, tended to be whimsical and romantic. Live entertainment was provided to the troops through traveling shows like the USO Camp Shows, Inc.; Camel Cigarette's famous "Camel Caravan" shows; and big bands and dances organized by local communities for the boys of the camp and the local girls to meet and mix. Magazines, pinups and 3.2 percent beer were all part of the culture of the era. A peek into Camp Campbell can be found in the camp's official newspaper, appropriately named *Retreat to Taps*, as its pages recorded off-duty time and events. (Retreat is a bugle call sounded at 5:00 p.m., signaling the lowering of the flag and the end of the duty day. Taps is a bugle call played at 10:00 p.m., signaling "lights out" and the end of the day. In between were five hours of off-duty.) The weekly camp paper featured a "cheesecake" picture of a Hollywood starlet on the front page; reviews of the latest movies playing at the four post theaters; news and gossip of the social doings in each unit; a cartoon or two of blatant risqué innuendo and suggestiveness that would probably not meet current Army standards of appropriateness; and news, much news, about all the many off-duty sports events and competitions. Since it was a time of racial segregation in the Army, news appropriate to the "Negro Troops"—such as a visit to the camp by "Miss Negro USA," social events held at the segregated Service Club and invitations to community events as far away as Nashville—were included. It was also a time of gender segregation, and news from the WAC detachment has its own curious interest: debates about the unfairness of WACs who were to be married being forced to wear their uniforms rather than traditional wedding gowns carried on for several months before the Army finally relented in favor of the gowns. But after 6 June 1944, the war took on a new gravity for the American people as Army casualties from the European Theater began to mount dramatically. The easy naïveté of the early camp years gave way to a deadly seriousness.

The world war was far from over as the last trained combat troops departed Camp Campbell. By early 1945, it was apparent that sufficient forces were available to see to the end of the war in Europe. In the Pacific Theater, however, the potential of an invasion of the Japanese mainland was another matter. Planners anticipated a need to shift troops from the victorious European Theater to the Pacific Theater. Such troops would need to be reorganized and retrained in the United States en route to the Pacific. Camp Campbell figured as a model location for testing the retraining

RETREAT to TAPS

VOL. I, No. 26   CAMP CAMPBELL, KENTUCKY   JULY 17, 1943

Anita Louise Wows Soldiers

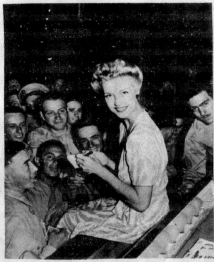

20th A.D.Photo

Lovely Anita Louise of the stage and screen entertains the soldiers at Service Club number 4. She autographed everything from G. I. shoelaces to books and letters to soldiers' girl friends.

Cubs Shut Out Post Team In Exhibition Game 11-0

The Chicago Cubs proved too much for a game Camp Campbell baseball team last Tuesday. The visitors defeated the soldiers 11-0 behind the effective pitching of Paul Erickson.

All Chicago players except "Peanuts" Lowery, centerfielder, joined in the 15-hit barrage, sending the soldiers to their fifth loss in 37 games played this year.

Manager Jimmy Reese of the Camp Campbell team made every effort to find the right combination of players to save the game, but the National Leaguers were just too good. Twenty-six soldiers took part in the game.

Stanky, Chicago's sensational rookie second baseman, opened the game by lining out a single to right. Martin walked, but Cavaretta, long a dependable Cub, brought Stanky home with a roaring triple to left-center. "Big Tom" Kelley, pitching for the soldiers, got by a tough spot in the second inning by fanning Erickson and forcing Martin to fly out with men on second and third.

In the third, the Cubs made it too hot for Kelley. Cavaretta was safe on Saccone's error. Dallessandro struck out, but Novikoff, known as the "Mad Russian," rammed a line double to left center scoring Cavaretta. Hernandez singled home, Novikoff took second on a wild pitch, and scored on Merullo's single to right.

Sergeant Zukowski took the mound in the fourth and was hammered for four hits and three runs. Dallessandro cleaned the bases with a triple after two singles and a walk had filled them.

Hernandez added the ninth run by homering over the left field fence in the fifth inning. The final two runs came in the eight and ninth innings as the result of errors.

Paul Erickson pitched eight innings allowing just four hits.

✚ Red Cross Grows With Camp Serving Soldiers Faithfully and Well

Beginning their work at Camp Campbell with only a field director and secretary, the American Red Cross services to the soldiers here has expanded and now includes a main office at Ohio avenue and 17th street, and three sub offices, one at the camp hospital, and one to serve each of the two armored divisions stationed at this post.

Rolland R. Ripple, field director detailed to the post, states that, "financial help to soldiers needing emergency furlough, verification of home conditions for the military, and per-

sonal services to the hospitalized men are the more important services given at this camp."

He added that much of the work, especially the help of the Grey ladies and the efforts in helping furnish and equip unit day rooms is a result of the co-operation of nearby Red Cross chapters working through their Camp Campbell council.

Mr. Gordon Cayce, Hopkinsville, is council chairman and holds regular meetings of the membership in the lounge of (Continued on page 7, column 2)

Retreat to Taps was a weekly paper published for the camp from 1942 to 1945.

and redeployment plan. Though the wheels for such a conversion were in motion at Camp Campbell, the use of the atomic bomb against Japan ended one need and opened the door for a final World War II mission, that of demobilizing the victorious Army.[34]

Demobilization itself was a large undertaking. Soldiers needed to be brought home from overseas and processed out of the Army in an organized fashion. Facilities and services in the camp had to remain in top shape; the requirements of housing, clothing and feeding soldiers had not diminished because of peace. Especially important for morale were sports and recreation facilities. The soldiers coming to out-process were not here to train, and hours needed to be fruitfully filled through the sometimes tedious process of leaving the army. The first out-processing unit was XVIII Corps, arriving in October 1945. The 5th Infantry Division arrived in September 1946. The last unit to out-process was the 3rd Infantry Division from March 1946 to May 1949.[35]

A Corps of Engineer study of the giant city-camps was made in 1947. The purpose of the survey was to determine which, if any, of the great camps was serviceable for continued use, if needed. Despite the wear and tear of the war years, Camp Campbell was deemed as useful and desirable. Perhaps not perceived at the time, changing circumstances in the postwar world would require use of this World War II camp in a new set of circumstances: the end of World War II and the beginning of the Cold War in 1948.

PUTTING THE CAMP IN OPERATION AND THE 1580TH SERVICE COMMAND UNIT

Construction at Camp Campbell proceeded with astonishing speed and efficiency throughout the spring and early summer of 1942. By July, about twenty-six million square feet of barracks, warehousing, motor pools and other facilities were completed. Following on the heels of construction that was nearing completion was the assignment of the first active-duty Army unit to be assigned to the camp: one officer and nineteen enlisted men who reported in at building T-1 as the cadre of the 1580th Service Command Unit on 1 July 1942.

Overall command of organizing and supplying the mobilization effort within the United States was under the Army Service Forces (ASF). It was one of only three autonomous commands reporting directly to the Army chief of staff, General George C. Marshall. The other autonomous commands were the Army Ground Forces Command (AGF) and the Army Air Forces Command (AAF). Lieutenant General Brehon Somervell, the same man who had directed the camp construction program during incremental mobilization, commanded the over 750,000 soldiers of the ASF. Somervell organized his command geographically along the same nine geographic boundaries used for the construction program, but now the nine corps commands were each commanded by a major general. Camp Campbell fell within the Fifth Corps area (Kentucky, Indiana and Ohio), headquartered in Columbus, Ohio. The Fifth Corps area was a 42,000-man organization commanded by Major General D.L. Van Voorhis (until 3 July 1942), Major General F.C. Wallace (until 2 December 1943) and Major General James L Collins (until the end of the war).[36]

Within each corps area, the further administration and running of the city-camps was assigned to a service command unit, which was commanded by a colonel who not only commanded the unit but also served as the post commander. The 1580th Service Command Unit was activated and assigned to Camp Campbell on 1 July 1942. Its first commander, and therefore the first post commander of Camp Campbell, was Colonel Guy W. Chipman. From "one and nineteen" on 1 July, the 1580th rapidly grew to a substantial organization of two hundred officers, five thousand enlisted soldiers and over two thousand civilians. The 1580th Service Command Unit functioned then as does the garrison command of today.

Colonel Chipman was typical of the high caliber of officer that was selected to command one of these complex, giant city-camps. A cadre of such officers was created by an order General George Marshall had issued in 1942 that, because of the rigors of training and combat, an officer who had reached the age of fifty-five and was not yet a general officer could no longer serve with combat troops. Like his cohort of over-fifty-five-year-old officers, Colonel Chipman had been commissioned from West Point in 1910. He had a distinguished career that spanned forty-two years. He is still one of the few Army officers to be a graduate of both the Army War College and the Naval War College. He and men like him who commanded these city-camps were proven leaders and managers. Colonel Chipman had also been part of the embryo Armor Forces Command at Fort Knox since 1941. In 1942, he was serving as a brigade commander in the newly activated 5th Armored Division. There was full expectation of his promotion to brigadier general shortly. General Marshall, however, would not make an exception to his order. As a result, Camp Campbell, designated as an armor training center, was fortunate to have a highly experienced and regarded armor officer as its first post commander.

Colonel Chipman served as the post commander until September 1943, when he was transferred to the Pacific Theater and commanded the Second

The World War II camp PX.

The parade field from 1942 to 1957 was located just inside Gate 4 on the site of the current Mahaffey Middle School.

Island Command under General MacArthur. Colonel Chipman was replaced by Colonel Herbert E. Taylor, a good friend and fellow cavalryman. Colonel Taylor commanded Camp Campbell until August 1946, when the Army deactivated the Army Service Forces. In the postwar years, Army forts and camps would be commanded by the senior officer present, usually the division commander of the unit assigned to the fort or camp.

In July 1942, when Colonel Chipman began organizing Camp Campbell, the Army selected the general staff officers and a commander for the soon-to-be-activated 12th Armored Division. Major General Carlos Brewer and his staff reported to the Command and General Staff College at Fort Leavenworth, Kansas, for a one-month staff preparation course. The new commander and his staff reported to Camp Campbell and occupied T-39 while newly drafted soldiers and recently trained officers and NCOs began to arrive to fill the new division. Pre-activation courses, minor range construction and the breaking in of the new barracks and mess halls filled the time in preparation for the division formal activation ceremony. The activation of the 12th and the formal activation of the camp occurred as a joint ceremony on 15 September 1942. The governor of Kentucky, Keen Johnson, was the guest of honor. Two grandsons, one granddaughter, one great-grandson and two great-great-grandsons of Brigadier General William Bowen Campbell were also present for the ceremony. The ceremony took place on the post parade field located just inside Gate 4, where Mahaffey Middle School is today.

THE 12TH AD, THE MTP AND THE TENNESSEE MANEUVERS: SEPTEMBER 1942– SEPTEMBER 1943

The organization and training of the 12th AD went according to script. The division received its fill of soldiers and was ready to begin training on 10 November 1942. The script for training was an Army document called the Master Training Program (MTP). The MTP for each branch of the Army laid out for the division cadre the individual through regimental training tasks required and a calendar by which to complete the training. The city-camps provided all that was necessary in the way of billets, supply, support and range facilities so that the cadre of the division could go about its task. The MTP schedule for the 12th Armor Division carried it through its initial training to September 1943, the prescribed ten months of training.

By the time the 12th AD was finishing its MTP program, the Army had developed a massive exercise area that would allow units that had trained up to regimental level at the city-camps the opportunity to conduct sophisticated division-size exercises to shake out division and corps command and control skills. The exercise area was called the Tennessee Maneuver Area. It was composed of the twenty-one counties east of Nashville, Tennessee. Activity in the maneuver area was under the direction of the 2nd U.S. Army headquartered in a high school gymnasium in Gallatin, Tennessee. The 2nd Army provided the command and control, the umpires and the evaluators for the maneuvers. Divisions and corps just out of MTP participated in a set of force-on-force exercises pitting two divisions of the Blue Force against two divisions of the Red Force. The grueling three-week exercise allowed the divisions to test their command and control skills and allowed the Army to evaluate and determine if a unit was ready to deploy overseas. The proximity of Camp Campbell to the Tennessee Maneuver Area made it a good place for some of the support units and units staging for the exercises. One unit that did stage for three days at Campbell Army Airfield prior to its participation in the maneuvers was the famous 506th Parachute Infantry Regiment of the 101st Airborne Division. The "Band of Brothers" enplaned at Camp Campbell Army Airfield for their jump into the maneuver area in June 1943.[37]

To prepare for their maneuvers, the men of the 12th AD participated in some preparatory exercises conducted by 2nd Army at Camp Campbell.

The 1942 armored division: shock, firepower and mobility.

20th Armored Division tanks on the firing line.

These innovative exercise scenarios allowed for off-post maneuvers that culminated on the camp's live-fire ranges. These large battalion-sized maneuvers were complex and challenging. The quality of today's tank, artillery and aerial bombing and strafing ranges in the north impact area of the camp owe their lineage to these pre-maneuvers exercises. The arrangement of the ranges and impact areas of today reflect the work that was done in 1943.

At the conclusion of the 12th's participation in the Tennessee Maneuvers, the 12th Armored Division was transferred from Camp Campbell to Camp Barkley, Texas, a sister armor city-camp, for more training prior to its embarkation to Europe. The experience of the 12th AD at Camp Campbell, likely because it was the first unit at the camp, was not recorded as a pleasant one. Much was made of the rawness of the training area, the severity of the weather and the lack of activity in the local towns. Neither Hopkinsville nor Clarksville had really prepared for the influx of off-duty soldiers, and they offered little in the way of entertainment. The USO, soon to be famous for its service clubs and hospitality, had only just been organized and had not yet established clubs in either town. The 12th AD's memories of the local towns and the camp were not fond. "No one shed any tears when we left the dust of Camp Campbell behind," was the closing tribute to the camp when chronicling the departure of the 12th AD in its official history.

INDIVIDUAL REPLACEMENTS AND THE 20TH ARMORED DIVISION: 15 MARCH 1943– DECEMBER 1944

By 1943, the War Department had settled the desired numbers, types and composition of the force needed to fight and win the war. Fourteen armored divisions was the required end strength of the armored forces. A replacement pool to sustain these divisions was required. Camp Campbell was selected as the place where individual replacement training for tankers, armored infantrymen and armored artillerymen would take place. A training division was organized to ready these replacements. The new training division, or "overseas replacement division," as it was called, for armored forces was designated the 20th Armored Division.

As the Armored Forces Command was undergoing a reorganizing of the structure of armored divisions in 1942–43, it activated the 20th Armored Division. The 20th AD was not "cut from whole cloth" as a brand-new division. The men and equipment of the 20th AD would come from the 8th AD. The 8th Armored Division, a division in formation under the old organization at Fort Knox, was ordered to Camp Campbell. The 8th Armored Division made the move as a tactical road march in the dead of the winter of 1942. It was recorded as a miserable experience by the soldiers who suffered through it. The 8th Armored Division closed into Camp Campbell in January 1943. Because of the larger organizational changes going on in the Armored Forces Command, the majority of the men and equipment of the 8th Armored Division were transferred into the about-to-be-activated 20th Armored Division. The command and control headquarters of the 8th Armored Division left Camp Campbell in March 1943. It moved to Camp Polk, Louisiana, and reestablished the 8th Armored Division with new units and equipment organized for the new 1943 armored division structure. Major General Stephen Henry, a dynamic leader and trainer, took charge of the newly activated 20th Armored Division at Camp Campbell on 15 March 1943. The division motto became "Beware the Ides of March."

On activation day, the 20th was fifteen thousand men strong. The camp designed for only twenty-three thousand men of one armored division and garrison support units was now expected to provide housing for two armored divisions *plus* the battalions from the 2nd Army that had been stationed at the camp. An appropriation for more housing was in the works. The short-term solution in the meantime was to build temporary hutments for the 20th AD soldiers. The 12th AD retained possession of T-39 as its headquarters and

Soldiers from the 20th Armored Division in the hutment area on the north end of the cantonment.

Series 800 barracks from 1st Street north. The 20th AD selected a building on Indiana Avenue near 41st Street for its headquarters, and the units occupied the north end of the cantonment to include where the hutments were built. A hutment was a very austere eight- by sixteen-foot bay of two- by four-foot frame with plywood and tarpaper siding.

The 20th AD trained more than thirty thousand replacements for the armored forces in 1943–44. The work was grueling, and the cycles were repetitive. Week after week, the cadre of the 20th saw their replacements off at the post rail siding destined for a war that seemed to be passing them by. The longevity of the 20th in the camp, however, had a profound and positive effect. Camp Campbell was more like a permanent home for the 20th than any transitory camp would have been. Much more work and care went into upgrading and maintaining the cantonment and range facilities than would have been the case if the 20th were a transitory division. Development and improvement of the range complexes—especially the infiltration course and the urban training range/complex called Hitlerville—were maintained and enhanced by a training cadre that used them repetitively.

The division commander, Major General Stephen Henry, was particularly attuned to recreation and off-duty relaxation as a morale builder for his

Hitlerville.

cadre and his replacement trainees. The service clubs, beer gardens and off-duty sports were given command priority: "When the day's training was done, dust-caked, perspiration soaked soldiers were able to relax in their coveralls, drink ice cold beer, listen to music and talk, always talk."[38] The commander's emphasis on team sport competition resulted in exceptional teams that performed exceedingly well in both military-sponsored and amateur civilian competitions. The baseball team won the Southeastern Service Tournament, defeated the All-Star Nashville City Team and was rated fourth in the National Amateur Athletic Union. The basketball team earned an invitation to the World's Professional Basketball Tournament in Chicago in 1944. Boxers from the 20th, Andy Anderson and Nick Tally, won the southeastern heavyweight Golden Gloves in 1943 and the light heavyweight Golden Belt in 1944, respectively.

As the cadre of the 20th AD was more or less hand-selected, it was noted after a short time that the average IQ score of the division cadre rose to 110, which was high enough to qualify one for Officer Candidate School.

The division took for itself the distinction of being the smartest division in the Army. Despite the distinction, however, being part of a training division got on many men's nerves. Most of the cadre thought of themselves as soldiers, and they wanted to be part of the "Great Crusade." They chafed at the role of "GI schoolteacher." In early 1944, however, the 20th Armored Division received new orders and was told to reorganize as a combat division and prepare for overseas deployment. Elated, the men of the division trained themselves to MTP standards. They were, after all, experts at those standards. Because it was so late in the war, the Army had closed the 2nd Army Tennessee Maneuvers. The 20th AD had to design its own pre-deployment exercise to replicate the challenge of the Tennessee Maneuvers. The local exercise included off-post maneuvers culminating on the live-fire ranges and the integration of over seventy-five close-air sorties. When the 20th Armored Division departed Camp Campbell in December 1944, the men were thrilled at their chance to participate in the Great Crusade. Their years at Camp Campbell had a significant and positive effect.

THE 26TH INFANTRY DIVISION, THE "YANKEE DIVISION": SEPTEMBER 1943–FEBRUARY 1944

As the 12th Armored Division pulled out of Camp Campbell, an established infantry division pulled in. This was the first of many changeovers between departing and arriving units. It was incumbent on the departing unit to "GI" the barracks and facilities to like-new standards for the arriving unit. It was the job of the 1580th to ensure those standards were met.

The arriving division was the 26th Infantry Division, nicknamed the "Yankee Division" because prior to the war it was the National Guard division of Massachusetts. It had a distinguished record of service in the First World War. Its headquarters had been in Boston. In the prewar years, it was the very symbol of Yankee service and patriotism. Because of the combination of history and geographic location, it tended to attract ambitious young men from the local elite colleges and areas that in many ways were above average. The division had a sort of highbrow taste that would be apparent in the pages of *Retreat to Taps* during the six months the division trained at Camp Campbell. For example, the division had brought with it from its previous assignment at Camp Gordon, Georgia, an art exhibit that featured over fifty paintings, sketches and photographs that had earned the praise of the Herbert Art Institute. The collection was displayed in Service Club 2, and a studio for soldier-artists was established. A soldier from HQ Company, Sergeant John Klein, was a professional organist and composer who gave very well-attended Brahms concerts and chapel performances.

The 26th Infantry was activated for federal service in the earliest days of incremental mobilization in late 1940. It was organized as a "square division" of two brigades of two regiments each. It had been assigned to six different camps before assignment to Camp Campbell. The 26th had provided individual officers and subordinate units for training and augmentation of other units for deployment to the Pacific Theater very early in the war. It underwent reorganization and retraining from a "square" to a "triangular" division, and it had been assigned the operational mission of patrolling the eastern seaboard in the early days of the war when Nazi U-boats and saboteurs presented a real threat. Its assignment to Camp Campbell was to allow the newly reorganized unit to finally conduct its required MTP training, participate in the Tennessee Maneuvers and deploy as soon as possible to England as part of the building invasion force. The 26th Infantry Division arrived at the camp as a cohesive unit.

The 26th Infantry Division arrived when the camp was beginning to achieve its full wartime maturity. The 1580th SCU had established itself as a superb garrison command. The 12th and the 20th Armored Divisions had developed the ranges and the maneuver areas to a high standard. In many ways, Hopkinsville and Clarksville had matured from small farming towns to local economies with a support infrastructure compatible with their "giant bachelor city" neighbor. The civilian workforce and civilian-operated concessions and services on the camp were fully staffed. In the larger culture, Hollywood had caught up with the camps and was nearing the height of its unique contributions to keeping up the morale of our boys. Reading issues of *Retreat to Taps* from this period of the camp's history is a chronicle of nearly weekly high-caliber USO shows; variety shows organized by Camel Cigarettes (the Camel Caravan) and General Electric Corporation; western rodeo shows; dances organized by the Special Services Branch, which brought in and chaperoned whole communities of young ladies from Nashville, Clarksville and Hopkinsville; and many, many weekly soldier-organized shows, sing fests and dances, dances, dances, featuring unit-level swing bands and jazz combos. Hollywood was releasing new movies with wartime themes, often romantic comedies that kept the camp theaters packed. The very active WAC detachments assigned to the camp were enthusiastic supporters and organizers of the dances. They were the

The "Camel Caravan" was a traveling troupe of performers sponsored by the Camel Cigarette Company. These shows ran the circuit of wartime mobilizations camps providing entertainment and, as you might expect, free Camel cigarettes for the troops.

female voices and presence in many of the home-spun soldier shows, and they even organized a professional WAC chorus that made appearances with organizations like the Cincinnati Symphony.

The experience of the 20th Armored Division and the 26th Infantry Division at Camp Campbell in the halcyon days of late 1943 and early 1944 has a quaint and giddy quality. It is almost too easy to say that camp life was fun. In context of the times, however, the real war had not yet begun. Certainly there was news from around the world and American casualties enough to remind the country of the grim reality of war, but those casualties were distributed widely across the population. Few Army divisions were yet committed to combat. Sicily, Italy; the campaigns of the Pacific; and above all the big invasion of Europe were yet to begin. America was in the in-between of the commitment made in the early days of incremental mobilization to ensure nothing but the best for our boys and the grim reality of the cost of real war. But in that in-between, it is worthwhile to ponder the impact of Camp Campbell on the local area. It is fair to say of the small-town, rural, tobacco-growing region along the Tennessee-Kentucky border, "Nothing like this ever happened around here before." Camp Campbell was a microcosm of a larger cultural change in America brought about by the war. There was the influx of strong and talented personalities into the community who built and ran the camp and who made their presence felt in the local economy, officers and men from all around the country, including the women of the WAC detachment and the Negro troops of the segregated units. These men and women met, socialized, intermingled and cross-fertilized the American

A 20th Armored Division–sponsored dance at a service club.

gene pool, so to speak. The inundation of popular culture that came to the area by way of the shows and personalities; the amateur sports that put Clarksville-Hopkinsville on the map; the bringing together of young men and women from all across America—it was a big camp. It made a big impact—and a lasting impact.

XX CORPS, "THE GHOST CORPS": APRIL 1943–FEBRUARY 1944

XXII CORPS: JANUARY 1944–DECEMBER 1944

A World War II Army corps headquarters was an organization capable of commanding and controlling a number of divisions. A corps headquarters had a lieutenant general (three stars), a robust staff of senior officers and a headquarters company. This nucleus of a corps headquarters numbered about six hundred men. A variable number of support units could be assigned to the corps headquarters to help it accomplish its mission of command and control. The mission of a corps was to command and sustain any number and types of divisions, normally three to five, that could be assigned to it. Divisions could "plug in" and "plug out" at a moment's notice and often did in combat. The purpose of a corps was to provide unity of direction and continuity of purpose in combat operations. At the beginning of the war, there was an attempt to fix corps headquarters organization. When fully augmented, in addition to the staff and headquarters company there could be an antiaircraft regiment, a cavalry regiment, two engineer combat regiments, a field artillery brigade, a tank destroyer group, a signal battalion and some combat service and combat service support units. By 1943, the Army had moved away from a fixed corps organization, and the organization of a corps became the essence of flexibility.

XX Corps was originally activated as IV Armor Corps. It activated at Camp Young, California, on 5 September 1942. Under the command of the IV Corps commander, Lieutenant General Walton Walker, Camp Young and the Desert Training Site grew into one of the largest training sites in Army history, encompassing most of the deserts of Southern California and western Arizona. After overseeing and participating in numerous large-scale, multi-division exercises, IV Armor Corps was transferred to Camp Campbell in March 1943. What came to Camp Campbell was the staff and headquarters company, about six hundred men. The corps was en route to the European Theater, and it came to Camp Campbell to polish its training and to participate in the Tennessee Maneuvers before deployment. From April through September, the staff trained at the camp. From 7 September through 4 November, a period of nine weeks, the corps participated in the Tennessee Maneuvers as one of the major commands, either the Blue Force command or the Red Force command, during two iterations of division-level exercises. Units that augmented the corps came from nearby camps. The corps commanded five divisions at various times during the exercise (26th, 30th, 75th, 83rd and 98th Infantry Divisions). Notably, one of those divisions, the 26th Infantry Division, is the same Yankee Division from Camp Campbell that joined the maneuvers for its three-week participation. Having spent time together with the staff of the 12th AD as well as the 26th ID while these units overlapped at Camp Campbell, peacetime relationships became wartime relationships. In the following year, both the 12th AD and the 26th ID fought in Europe under the command and control of the XX Corps.

Whatever IV Armor Corps lacked in the way of the artistic and cultural talents of the 26th ID and in the athletic prowess of the 20th AD, there was, nonetheless, one really big event sponsored by the corps that set it apart from everyone else at the camp. When still in California in 1942, IV Armor Corps had provided the technical assistance and battlefield background for the making of the Columbia Pictures classic *Sahara*, starring Humphrey Bogart. The film came ready for release just as the corps was about to celebrate its first anniversary. In appreciation for its assistance, Columbia Pictures arranged for the world premiere of *Sahara* to be held at Camp Campbell. A special outdoor amphitheater was constructed on the south end of the cantonment area. Hollywood came with its best, to include Bogart, Lulubelle the M3 Lee tank and a stage show. Twenty-five thousand soldiers attended the event, which was open to the local civilian community. Only a few days later, the corps deployed to the maneuvers.

Upon its return from the field, the corps was officially renamed the XX Corps. The Army had decided that "a corps is a corps is a corps" and dropped the idea of specialized armor corps. The new patch was the result of a corps-wide contest. After sewing on their new shoulder insignia, a brief period of recovery from the maneuvers and a period of time for stateside furlough, the men of the newly designated corps began the process of POM (Preparation for Movement). The corps departed Camp Campbell in February 1944 destined for Europe.

As XX Corps pulled out of Camp Campbell, the Army activated the XXII Corps. The XXII did not come from a previous assignment but was put together from scratch and birthed at Camp Campbell. It was commanded by Major General Henry Terrell. Terrell had seen the 90th ID through its MTP and stateside training. He had just relinquished command of the 90th Infantry Division as that division departed for England. The principal staff officers and members of the headquarters company arrived over the next month from various assignments around the Army. As the staff was organizing and beginning its training, several officers were selected to attend month-long courses at the Command and General Staff College.

The new corps fit in with the routine of the camp. The 20th Armored Division, now very well established as the longest-serving unit at the camp, assisted with soldier training. As the corps headquarters matured over time, those units that would be assigned to augment the corps were also assigned to the camp. Several tank destroyer battalions, a mechanized cavalry reconnaissance squadron, a Military Police company and the headquarters and headquarters battery of the XXII Corps Artillery were joined together as the corps began to develop teamwork. An odd and new experimental unit was also assigned to the corps. It was called the 8th Machine Records Unit (8th MRU). The unit's equipment included several tractor-trailer trucks and some new punch card machines from a company called International Business Machine (IBM). The mission of the unit was to assist the Corps G1 section with personnel management. The IBM-Army effort was an early attempt to automate personnel records.

XXII Corps trained at Camp Campbell for eleven full months. Additional training was not deemed necessary, and the war was rapidly winding toward a conclusion. It was ready for overseas deployment in February 1945. It got to Europe as Germany was collapsing. The corps fought the last two months of the war in Europe, 31 March to the last day of the war, 7 May. Interestingly, the corps commanded three of the four airborne divisions in Europe: 82nd Airborne, 31 March–30 April; 101st Airborne, 1 April–6 April; and 17th Airborne, 27 April–7 May.

14TH ARMORED DIVISION (LAST MAJOR COMBAT UNIT TO TRAIN AT CAMP CAMPBELL): FEBRUARY 1944–OCTOBER 1944

The 14th Armored Division, like XX Corps and the 26th ID, came to Camp Campbell well after its activation and MTP from another mobilization camp. The 14th was activated at Camp Chaffee, Arkansas, in November 1942. Its commander, Major General Vernon Pritchard, had taken the 14th from MTP and through several grueling weeks of exercises as part of the Tennessee Maneuvers from late November 1943 to January 1944. After a successful conclusion of the maneuvers, the 14th AD conducted a tactical road march from the vicinity of Gallatin, Tennessee, to Camp Campbell. The 26th ID had not yet vacated the barracks, so the 14th AD went into administrative bivouac until the 26th cleared out in early February.

The training that the 14th AD conducted at Camp Campbell became known as "post-maneuver training." Although the division was trained for deployment by all Army standards, the sequencing of forces into England and then cross-Channel into France had to be taken into consideration. When the 14th AD came to Camp Campbell, it was yet six months until D-Day. When the 14th left Camp Campbell, the invasion was six months in progress. The 14th was sequenced for deployment to hit Europe running. In the meantime, not a moment of valuable training time was lost.

As stated in the division's Training Memo #7, "The purpose of post maneuver training is for final preparation for battle; for the perfecting of the technique of individuals and units; to correct deficiencies noted in maneuvers. This program is divided into three phases, each of which is estimated to require two months for completion." The outline of the three phases was: 1, individual skill proficiency; 2, small unit proficiency; and 3, training of larger, reinforced units (battalion live-fire exercises). In between the lines, during phase 1 the division took advantage of proximity to Fort Knox, the armor center, to send soldiers for short courses, especially soldiers with technical skills such as communications, mechanics and ordnance. During phase 2, the focus was on gunnery and small unit tactics, with extensive use made of the now well-developed ranges in the maneuver area. During the final phase, reinforced battalion maneuver and live-fire were conducted.

Several major camp-wide events occurred during the tenure of the 14th AD. On 7 and 8 March 1944 the chief of staff of the Army, the man who had recommended the site of the Tennessee-Kentucky Armor Camp back in July 1941 as a hedge on the continuing incremental mobilization program, came to inspect the camp and training. On 15 June 1944, the camp celebrated National Infantry Day. The armored infantrymen of the 20th AD and the 14th AD were highlighted in live-fire and static display demonstrations. A review on the parade field and a ball at the field house (Dryer Field House) completed the celebration. The celebration was extremely well attended by citizens of Clarksville and Hopkinsville and seems to have cemented a growing relationship between the camp and the host civilian communities. Shortly after the National Infantry Day, Major General Pritchard gave up command of the 14th to General A.C. Smith, who would take the trained 14th Armored Division to combat. In August, the division culminated its training with a division-wide live-fire exercise lasting three full days.

In August, aware that deployment was just around the corner, the division took advantage of the opportunity to take final leaves and furloughs. In September, training became a constant series of inspections as the division began its POM. The advance party left on 21 September. By 8 October, the 14th AD had closed on Camp Shanks, New York, a well-worn camp by this time that served as the port of embarkation for units deploying to Europe.

POWS: JULY 1943–APRIL 1946

American and British success in the 1942–43 campaign in North Africa resulted in a substantial number of POWs. The Geneva Convention required captors to provide a level of care for POWs similar to the level of care given to their soldiers. The harsh environment and lack of infrastructure in North Africa presented a serious obstacle to housing POWs. The only other "friendly terrain" available in Europe in 1943 was Great Britain, which was hardly a satisfactory solution either. Staging soldiers and supplies for the coming invasion left little room for POWs, and the closeness of the continent would make escape attempts tempting.

The solution to the POW problem was to move them to the United States. The huge convoys bringing soldiers and supplies to Great Britain were empty and available for POW transport on the return trip. The United States had space, plenty of it. The obstacle of the Atlantic Ocean negated any possibility of an escape return to Germany and the fight.

The mission of housing POWs in the United States was given to the Army Service Forces, that autonomous command that was responsible for running all the giant city-camps. In the short term, 72 POW camp locations were identified in early 1943. By the war's end, there were 511 POW camps providing housing for 400,000 German and Axis country POWs.

Camp Campbell was designated as one of those early POW camp locations. The design of the POW compounds was standardized, and construction diagrams were provided to contractors just as was the Series 700–800 cantonment camp plan. Three standardized compound facilities were built

A guard tower at POW Compound 2.

within the Camp Campbell cantonment area. One facility was located at the south end of the cantonment near the intersection of Desert Storm Avenue and Mabry Road, the second was located where Hammond Heights Housing Area is now near the intersection of Reed and Forrest Avenues and the third was located near the present location of Lincoln Elementary School. A total of three thousand prisoners were transferred here beginning 24 July 1943. The MP company of the 26th Infantry Division that was training at the camp at that time was detailed to go TDY (on temporary duty) to the East Coast to pick up the POWs and escort them to the camp. The Army Services Command provided the command and control of the POW camps by forming MP guard battalions. The unit assigned to Camp Campbell was the 1539th SCU. The commander, Lieutenant Colonel Carl B. Byrd, was a member of the Camp Campbell staff. His unit was made of three MP companies. Those who were assigned to MP guard duty tended to be older soldiers or those physically incapacitated soldiers who could not deploy overseas. In the latter part of the war, soldiers who had recovered from wounds but could not redeploy overseas were trained and assigned as guards.

The German and Italian POWs were a mixed lot. There were some who were ardent Nazis and fascists. That kind was identified and segregated early in one compound that was designated for troublesome prisoners. POWs were given the option to work. According to the Geneva Convention, a prisoner had the right to refuse to work, but a very large percentage of the Camp Campbell prisoners chose to work. By law, their work could not directly aid the war effort, but their labor could be used to replace the labor performed by citizens who had to leave the local area to serve in the war. POWs were compensated for their work.

Work available to the POWs came in three categories. POWs could work at the Station Hospital. Such work included duties as ward boys, dental assistants, groundskeepers and KP in the hospital kitchens and cafeteria. POWs could work as a labor force in support of the post engineer and quartermaster. They could work in carpenter shops, the ration breakdown point, the supply warehouses and on post cleanup and beatification projects. A third labor program was called "farming out." Local farmers could hire POWs to aid in dairy, tobacco and grain harvest labor. Nationwide, other industries could hire POW labor in limited circumstances. Stone quarry and timber were two such industries. Locally, a farmer could contract POW labor at a rate of $1.20 to $2.00 per day per POW. The farmer was required to provide transportation for the POWs and their guard. The Army provided the noon meal. In all cases, the POWs received

German POWs working on a local farm.

compensation. Sometimes it was cash; sometimes it was in the form of coupons redeemable at the POW PX.

Life in the compound was disciplined but not harsh. The POW life was luxurious enough to cause resentment by members of the Clarksville American Legion, who became quite vocal, as recorded in the local press beginning in April 1944. The resentment was that the POWs were living "the good life" while American boys were suffering and dying on the increasingly active worldwide battlefield. The complaint was not too far from wrong. Despite the deprivation of a prisoner's life, much care was taken of the POWs. Inspections by the International Red Cross were scheduled, and weekly mail privileges ensured contact with families back home. Each compound had a well-stocked PX. German or American movies were available nightly. POWs produced two theatricals per month; had a symphony orchestra and a swing band; produced piano recitals and band concerts; and had access to a phonograph record program, providing the latest tunes available on record. An approved German newspaper was available daily, and the POWs produced their own weekly newspaper, *Der Neue Weg* (the *New Way*). Organized sports were available after duty, as were language courses, vocational classes and home study college courses from the University of Chicago.

There were escapes from captivity. The local press recorded them as they occurred. In all cases (about a dozen instances), the escapes occurred while the men were farmed-out, not from the compounds. The prisoners were recovered in a matter of several days to a week. In almost every case, the recovery was due to the POW turning himself in to authorities after a hiatus. It appears that most of the time, the escape was not an attempt to repatriate with Germany but an attempt to temporarily escape the dreariness of POW life, hopefully in the arms of willing and amiable company. There was but one recorded incident of a POW escape coming to a bad end. On 22 January 1944, POW Josef Redinger was discovered in the vicinity of the Pembroke train station (a local town ten miles southeast of the camp). While attempting to avoid recapture, he was shot while fleeing. There were four other POW deaths, all from natural causes. All five POWs who died while prisoners here are buried in a small, well-maintained plot located on Clarksville Base near Mabry Road.

At war's end, all POWs began a process of repatriation, as was required by the Geneva Convention. None could stay here; they had to return to their home countries. Those who were deemed reliable and "pro-American" were repatriated first in order to help and support the postwar military government in the Allied Zone with police and constabulary duties. Others were transferred from Camp Campbell and underwent a period of re-education before going back. Not all went directly home. There were provisions that some were kept in a detainee status and made to work repairing war damage in Allied countries for a period of time before their eventual full release. In retrospect, through the lens of the Cold War, and even if not that through the lens of humanity and decency, the good and perhaps even "luxurious" care afforded to the POWs in America paid dividends in the postwar world when many Germans had to take a stand for the West or for the East in the coming superpower confrontation of the Cold War.

WOMEN IN THE GIANT BACHELOR CITY

Though it was a "giant bachelor city," there were many women who were associated with the camp. Some were associated in traditional ways, and some were associated in a new way. The most traditional were the wives of Regular Army senior officers and NCOs who did not live on the camp, as they may well have on a more traditional Army post, but who nonetheless filled their traditional roles at formal social affairs on the camp and within the civilian communities in which they resided. The women of the Red Cross

The Red Cross office at the Station Hospital.

filled their traditional and well-established role of providing emergency notification for soldiers and their families and assisting with patient care in the hospital, as well as assisting with the running of unit day rooms and other canteen activities. Almost half of the two thousand civilian workers on the camp were women. Their jobs included staffing the unit PXs, working in the libraries and post office, secretarial duties throughout the camp, working for the Special Services Branch (the forerunner to the modern MWR) and working at some of the civilian concessions on the camp, such as the Planters Bank. These many women who were associated with the camp did not live on the camp, nor were they members of the Army.

There was one group of women, however, who were fulfilling a traditional role, who were in the Army and who resided on the camp. These were the women of the U.S. Army Nurse Corps. Congress authorized the U.S. Army Nurse Corps in 1901. Army nurses, all of whom were commissioned officers,

U.S. Army nurses at the Station Hospital.

were assigned to the Station Hospital from the activation of the camp. By mid-1943, there were over sixty Army nurses assigned to the Station Hospital. The nurses were unmarried and were accorded bachelor officer housing in the vicinity of the hospital. Their status as medical professionals and as commissioned officers provided privacy and distance from the robust social life of the enlisted soldiers recorded in the pages of *Retreat to Taps*.

What was very new and very nontraditional to the Army was the Women's Army Corps, the WAC. The WACs began as the Women's Auxiliary Army Corps (WAAC), authorized by Congress under the Rogers Bill signed into law on 15 May 1942. The Rogers Bill was the work of the first woman elected to Congress, Representative Edith Nourse Rogers (R, MA). Her interest and intent was to provide an opportunity for women to serve in noncombat positions in order to free men for combat roles. Formally, the WAAC was intended as a group of women trained to military standard to serve as an auxiliary force with the Army in any capacity that did not require the use of arms. The goal was ambitious: to replace able-bodied male soldiers assigned to noncombat but necessary duty with women for those jobs "which women can do better than men" and also for noncombat duties for which, when properly trained, "women can do as well as men."

The idea of women in uniform was very controversial at the time. In the 1940s, there was a profound cultural predisposition against women serving. The bill languished in Congress for months and then squeaked through the House of Representatives and passed the Senate by only a narrow margin.

The WAAC and the WAC program was commanded and controlled by the Army Service Forces. These WAAC and WAC units were then allocated to the corps commands of the ASF. Women assigned to Camp Campbell wore the shoulder patch of the Fifth Corps Area Command of the ASC. At Camp Campbell, they were assigned to the post commander and commander of the 1580th SCU. Three companies of WAACs were assigned to Camp Campbell: the 48th WAAC Post Headquarters Company (4 March 1943), the 165th WAAC Post Headquarters Company (24 April 1943) and a third company (27 May 1943). All three companies were consolidated into the 3563rd Service Unit, WAAC, in July 1943.

The WAAC was, as the title implied, an auxiliary unit to the Army. The auxiliary arrangement soon proved unsatisfactory. As auxiliaries, the WAACs were denied several key benefits. The most important of these benefits included the death gratuity accorded to members of the Armed Forces and the protected status as POWs under the Geneva Convention. As women began to be deployed overseas to Africa and Europe, these became real concerns. Equal pay, leave and allowances also proved to be problematic. In order to correct those imbalances, the Rogers Bill provisions were amended so that the WAAC was converted to be included in the Regular Army. The name was changed to delete the "auxiliary" status to the plain Women's Army Corps, or WAC. The official change took effect on 12 August 1943. A special swearing-in ceremony for the new WACs was held at Camp Campbell on 1 September 1943. Shortly

The WAC detachment forming for retreat.

thereafter, the name of the unit at Camp Campbell became WAC Section of the 1580th Service Unit.

The WAACs/WACs lived on the camp in Series 800 barracks, just like the men. Officers were accorded a female bachelor officers' quarters. The only modifications to the Series 800 WAC barracks were to the latrines in order to provide for private commode and shower stalls. Curtains, naturally, adorned the windows. The WAC area was similar to any other company area. In addition to the barracks, a recreation building, headquarters and supply building and WAC mess hall were provided. Facilities in the WAC area included a beauty parlor. The WAC area was off-limits to males except for after hours, remembering a very strict curfew of 2200 hours (10:00 p.m.), when male escorts were allowed to return their dates to the barracks front porch. Rules outlined in *Retreat to Taps* emphasized that the return-to-barracks escort should not take advantage of the privilege by lingering and overstaying his welcome, lest the privilege be denied to all in the future.

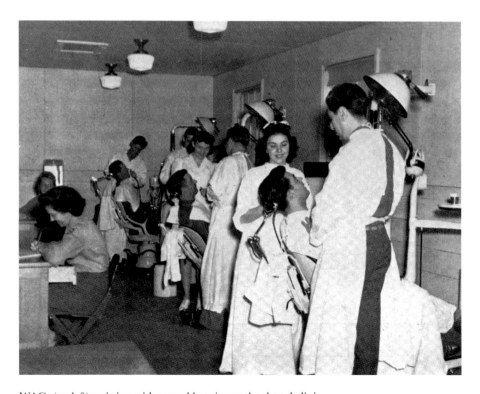

WACs (on left) assisting with record keeping at the dental clinic.

While the WACs did live communally, they were assigned duty positions as individuals. Their varied duty positions were spread throughout the camp. A program from a celebration of the first anniversary of the WACs at the camp listed 44 different jobs to which the two hundred women of the unit were assigned. The list was as diverse as ambulance driver to court reporter to lab technician to tank parts assembler. By the end of the war, of the 648 jobs identified in the Army, women were qualified to serve in 400 of them.

The social life of the enlisted women of the WAC section was well documented in *Retreat to Taps*. Like other units, the WAC section had its own news and gossip column that told of internal WAC news. Word from former unit members who had been transferred, visits from family members, attitudes toward policies affecting the WACs, impending marriages, etc., were typical of the gossip. The paper announced several marriages between WACs and soldiers. Dances, picnics and field trips to places such as Mammoth Cave National Park were remarkably regular activities. Outside the gossip column, there was much news about WACs participating in soldier-produced theatricals, concerts and sing-fests sponsored by the all-male units at the camp in need of female actors and voices. In addition to lending their talents to these productions, the WACs put together their own thirty-member WAC Chorus, which performed numerous times on national radio from Nashville on radio station WLAC. As mentioned earlier, the WAC Chorus was good enough to perform with the Cincinnati Civic Chorus and Symphony Orchestra and did so on national radio for the May Musical Festival in May 1944.

The WACs were justifiably proud of their contributions at Camp Campbell. Army-wide, the WAAC/WAC program was deemed a success by the hierarchy. WACs at Camp Campbell boasted that they were doing "man-sized jobs and doing them as well and in many cases better than the men who formerly occupied the same positions." The women proudly said of themselves, "The old-time army term 'goldbricking' is non-existent in this new army of skirts." In April 1946, the Army deactivated the Army Service Forces, the 1580th Service Command and, with it, the WAC section. The WAC, as a corps, remained part of the active Army until its deactivation in 1974, when women were transferred to regular Military Occupations Specialties (MOSs) jobs in the Army. While there were individual WACs who served at Fort Campbell and even in the division prior to 1974, no post–World War II WAC unit or section was ever again assigned to Camp Campbell or Fort Campbell.

DEMOBILIZATION:
12 MAY 1945–30 JUNE 1947

The official dates for the demobilization of the World War II Army are 12 May 1945 to 30 June 1947. At the end of the war in Europe, there were 8.3 million men and women on active duty. The Army planned to reduce forces between the fall of Germany and the concluding campaign against Japan to a force of 6.3 million. Once Japan was defeated, the plan was to draw down to a force of 1.3 million. The demobilization was a complicated process. There were issues of grand strategy to be sorted out between the State Department and the War Department concerning national objectives and security, priorities and postwar commitments. There was the issue of how to keep recruiting going strong enough so that new recruits, volunteers, could replace the long-serving drafted combat veterans on postwar occupation duty. There were issues among Congress and the War and Navy Departments over who should control the pace and scope of demobilization: those who mobilized the military (Congress) or those who fought the war (the military departments). The World War II military were citizen-soldiers who had been drafted into service. Once the war was over, there was a huge clamor, several times erupting into GI protests in both Europe and the Pacific, to get soldiers and sailors home as fast as possible. The concluding sentence of the Army's official history of personnel demobilization observed, "When future scholars evaluate the history of the United States during the first-half of the twentieth century they will list World War II demobilization as one of the cardinal mistakes."

The story of demobilization at Camp Campbell is a microcosm of the larger story. The last of the major combat units departed the camp in January 1945. During the six-month period between January and May, when the official demobilization began, the 1580th, the Station Hospital, the WAC section and the civilian workforce began to draw down. Some effort was made to prepare for restationing and redeployment, a plan that would provide camps for troops being redeployed from Europe to the Pacific, but the plan never went beyond staff planning. The unexpectedly rapid collapse of Japan in August 1945 because of the atomic bomb obviated the need to pursue implementation of that plan. There was much anticipation in the camp for demobilization. Everyone wanted to go home, but many at the camp needed to stay to administer the camp and oversee and assist units in the demobilization process.

Between May and August, the Army began to draw down forces in Europe that would not be needed for Japan. One of those units was the famous XVIII Airborne Corps. Invasion plans for Japan did not include a need for the command and control provided by an airborne corps. The XVIII Airborne Corps arrived at Camp Campbell in June and completed its demobilization process in six months, by November 1945. The process for a unit to demobilize included an equipment turn-in and personnel out-processing. Equipment turn-in involved technical inspections and repairs at the camp if required. Serviceable equipment was destined for depots as war surplus stocks for possible reissue if the need arose. Personnel out-processing, the last step, included records processing, transition counseling, physical exams, a uniform for the trip home, finance out-processing and a departure ceremony. When individual out-processing began, those with the highest points were the first to go. This created an interesting leadership challenge, as the high-point men tended to be the most senior. First sergeants, supply sergeants and mess sergeants went first. Needless to say, there was not much use made of the range complexes, but commanders were required to keep soldiers gainfully employed and provided with athletic, recreation, intellectual and spiritual opportunities. The Special Services Branch had its hands full providing such opportunities.

The war in the Pacific ended while the XVIII Airborne Corps was completing its out-processing (August 1945). The Army demobilization goals suddenly moved from reducing the Army to 6.5 million men to an accelerated reduction down to 1.3 million men. The 5th Infantry Division arrived at the camp in November 1945 as the XVIII Corps was closing out. The 5th out-processed from November 1945 to September 1946, a period of ten months. While the 5th was out-processing, the Army was undergoing a serious reorganization at the senior level. A part of that reorganization included the deactivating of the Army Service Forces, which had commanded the camps, the POW internment, the WACs and so much more of the stateside Army. Under the new plan, territorial control of the United States was vested in a number of Armies; the camp now fell under the jurisdiction of the 2nd U.S. Army. In the new command arrangement, the 5th Infantry Division commander, Major General Jens A. Does, became the camp commander. Command and administration was no longer separated from the senior commander present. A new position, the deputy post commander, was established and became a subordinate to the commanding officer. The deputy post commander saw to the administration of the garrison much the same as the 1580th commander had during the war.

As the 5th Infantry Division completed its out-processing, the 3rd Infantry Division moved in beginning in September 1946 as the last of the demobilizing units. It did not take long for the 3rd to out-process its remaining wartime soldiers. By April 1947, most of the 3rd was gone. The headquarters of the 3rd ID moved to Fort Benning, Georgia, and that division was rebuilt as a Regular Army division for continued active duty. As of May 1947, just about the time the Army ended the formal demobilization program, the total strength in the camp drifted down to only 1,712 soldiers. These soldiers performed as a skeleton crew to keep the camp operational. The civilian workforce of about as many civilians worked mostly in the second and third echelon maintenance facilities to repair and recover equipment. The strength of the camp remained that remarkably low until March 1948.

In March 1947, the Corps of Engineers conducted a study of each of the giant bachelor city-camps to make a determination if any of them had the potential for continued service and to provide an estimate of the cost to provide housing for married officers and the top three grades of NCO. The survey was favorable for Camp Campbell. It was determined that a total of $48.5 million had been spent thus far on the camp. It was rated favorable in all key infrastructure with the exception of proximity to a major city for recreational support. It was deemed that mobilization housing of the Series 800 type could support a soldier population of 21,552, one division. The cost of providing officer and senior NCO housing was estimated at $27 million.

While Camp Campbell lingered in the twilight of World War II, new and ominous events were taking place around the world. The wartime alliance with the Soviet Union was turning into a dangerous postwar competition. Mao's Communist victory in China in 1948 was shocking. Unrest throughout the world stoked by the Soviets presented an existential threat to the West. Winston Churchill had used the phrases "Iron Curtain" and "Cold War" to describe the new strategic situation. As President Truman formulated a response to the new dire international situation, the story of the city of Fort Campbell was about to enter a new chapter, that of the national defense city.

Chapter 5

THE NATIONAL DEFENSE CITY

1948–1965

As the population of Camp Campbell dwindled to next to nothing by 1948, it certainly must have looked like a well-worn relic and maybe even something more like a ghost town. The majority of the barracks, theaters, chapels, mess halls and sports fields were unoccupied, unused, padlocked and showing the effects of weather and neglect on top of the results of hard use from the war years.

There were great hopes for a new international order in the immediate aftermath of the Great Crusade. Enemies crushed, the wartime Army of 8 million had demobilized down to a strength of 1.3 million men and women. The United Nations had been established. Peace and international cooperation seemed assured. Such, however, would not be the case. Between 1945 and 1948, a new political reality took hold: an ideological confrontation between the USSR and the USA that would persist for the next fifty years. It was called, from its earliest days, the Cold War.

The Cold War had profound effects on what was to become of old Camp Campbell. The first effect was a result of the development and use of nuclear weapons in World War II, a development that would define the dangers the Cold War when the Soviets stole our atomic secrets and became a nuclear power too. In 1946, however, the United States was the only nation that possessed nuclear weapons. A plan to manage and store nuclear weapons, the Atomic Energy Act of 1946, was developed. One feature of the plan was to select a number of sites spread across the United States to safely store the nuclear arsenal. One of the thirteen top-secret nuclear weapons storage and modification sites selected was to be located on Camp Campbell. It was called Site Charlie until it was given the name Clarksville Base. Construction began in 1947, and the facility was operational by 1949. As the Cold War intensified, the importance of Clarksville Base and nuclear deterrence grew too. It remained an active site until 1965. It was decommissioned from 1965 to 1969 and returned to the control of Fort Campbell.[39]

The second profound effect of the Cold War was that it caused the nation to focus on defense as the most important government and national priority. So important was this purpose to defend the country from the threat of Soviet domination that some historians refer to the change in focus of the government as the establishment of a "national security state." The National Defense Act of 1947 established new and powerful government agencies to accomplish this new purpose. The act consolidated the old War Department into a modern Department of Defense (DOD) headquartered at the world's largest building at the time, the Pentagon. The act consolidated the separate Army Department and Navy Department and established the Joint Chiefs of Staff. It established a National Security Council (NSC) to advise the president on matters of national strategy. It established a new Department of the Air Force and consolidated all intelligence-gathering agencies into one Central Intelligence Agency (CIA), which was also given the authority to conduct covert operations outside the United States. Small parts of the bigger national security state were the many places like Camp Campbell that would become "national defense cities."[40]

The third effect, and perhaps the most profound for the city's history, was the change of the Army's sociology. The Cold War required a new type of Army. The old model relied on a small, professional Regular Army that would serve as a nucleus for expanding a giant citizen army, if required. The Soviet and Communist threat in the Cold War was ever present and required an Army that was ever ready and ever vigilant. This larger, professional, full-time Army required a large cadre of officers and NCOs, and it required a draft to keep it manned. Selective Service was reestablished in 1948 and became a fact of life for all male citizens until the advent of the all-volunteer Army in 1974. The change in sociology was that this larger, full-time Army was not about to be a bachelor Army like that of World War II. The bachelor Army gave way to a married Army. The national defense city became home, therefore, to what has sometimes been referred to as the "national defense family": Army husband, Army wife and Army children (often called "Army brats" but not in a pejorative sense), who each had a role to play and sacrifices to make in the larger national and Army effort.

Housing, schools, healthcare, family recreation, shopping, auto care, etc., became new and essential requirements to sustain this new full-time Army family. Old Camp Campbell, the giant bachelor city, required a significant upgrade to accommodate this new, full-time and professionalizing Army and the many families that were to become part of the national defense city.[41]

The confrontation between the USSR and the United States waxed and waned from 1948 to 1965. The city of Fort Campbell was center stage to the hotter end of the Cold War. Twice the intensity broke into shooting wars: Korea (1950–53) and the Vietnam advisory years (1960–65). Soldiers and families from Fort Campbell were affected by both. The nuclear confrontation between the two superpowers was profoundly dangerous. Just how important a participant Fort Campbell was in the nuclear confrontation is often overlooked. Fort Campbell became home to a top-secret nuclear weapons storage and modification site from 1948 to 1965. At one time, about one-third of the nation's nuclear arsenal was stored at this facility. Activities here were of priority interest to the Soviet KGB and the GRU. The FBI maintained an office in Clarksville to check just such interest. The most dangerous of all nuclear events in the early Cold War was the Cuban Missile Crisis (October 1962). Weapons and bombs stored at the facility were prepared for operation and loaded on transporters at the gates of Clarksville Base to be taken on the three-mile trip to Campbell Army Airfield so that bombers of the Strategic Air Command could load them into their bomb racks—the last step before nuclear release. President Kennedy's nuclear saber rattling was not mere rhetoric.[42]

THE AIRBORNE COMES TO FORT CAMPBELL: 1948–1967

From 1948 to 1967, Fort Campbell was successively the home of two of the Army's post–World War II Airborne Divisions, the 11th Airborne Division (1948–56) and the 101st Airborne Division (1956–67). In the years after World War II, Fort Campbell ceased to be a training center for armor units and developed a distinctive "airborne/air assault culture'" that it has retained to the present. The 101st Airborne Division was deployed to Vietnam from 1967 to 1972, but it did return to Fort Campbell after the deployment. All of the major combat units assigned to the city since 1948 have had a "vertical envelopment" mission, an Army term that means a unit is trained to maneuver against the enemy through the air either by the traditional parachute (airborne) or the more modern helicopter (air assault).

The 11th Airborne and the 101st Airborne of the early Cold War years each represented the evolving Cold War Army in distinct ways. The 11th Airborne Division retained its World War II organization, tactics, equipment and mission. When General Douglas MacArthur took command of UN forces in Korea in 1950, he asked for an airborne division to be deployed as part of his command. There were only two airborne divisions on active duty, the 82nd Airborne and the 11th Airborne. The Pentagon would not give up the 82nd Airborne Division because of a fear that the action in Korea was merely a Communist deception for a bigger attack on Europe. The 82nd Airborne Division was a key part of the nation's strategic reserve. The only other airborne division on active duty, the 11th, was just moving into Camp Campbell, and it was seriously under strength. The best that could be mustered was one regiment. The 187th Infantry Regiment was the regiment selected. The regiment was beefed up with additional logistics, artillery and combat support platoons. It was put under the command of a one-star general officer and became a separate Airborne Regimental Combat Team (187th ARTC). It was sent to Korea to fight. In Korea, the Army fought a grueling ground war with mostly World War II weapons and tactics. The Korean War was expensive and became unpopular. Disentangling the United States from the effort was a major campaign issue in the presidential election of 1952. The cadre and non-deployed regiments of the 11th Airborne Division remained at Fort Campbell, prepared for war, and were one of six active divisions tasked to augment basic training for newly drafted soldiers as individual replacements for units deployed in Korea. Significantly, the 11th Airborne Division also established an Airborne School at Fort Campbell to augment basic airborne training conducted at Fort Benning, Georgia. An Airborne School operated here on and off from 1950 to 1955 under the supervision of the 11th Airborne Division. The school then became the responsibility of the 101st Airborne Division from 1956 to 1962. Over thirty thousand basic airborne students graduated from the school.

The course of the Cold War turned in the post-Korea era (1953), when newly elected President Eisenhower re-crafted U.S. defense policy to take advantage of the power and relatively less expensive use of nuclear deterrence to shrink the need for relatively more expensive large conventional forces to counter the international Soviet threat. This change in policy greatly enhanced the Air Force and the Navy budgets with their new nuclear delivery systems of bombers, aircraft carriers and submarines,

Fort Campbell Airborne School.

but it greatly diminished the role, purpose and budget of the Army. The policy was called the "New Look." NATO allies expected the United States to bolster forces in Europe to visibly guarantee the credibility of the U.S. nuclear deterrence promise. The 11th Airborne was caught up in the global repositioning of forces called "Operation Gyroscope." The 11th was scheduled for deployment to Europe as part of a demonstration of the U.S. nuclear guarantee. In early 1956, the entire 11th Airborne Division moved to Augsburg, Federal Republic of Germany. This, of course, left Fort Campbell nearly empty, as it had been in 1947. This was a great concern for local citizens who had in many ways become dependent on a growing economic relationship between the post and the local economy. The void was to be filled by the reactivation of the 101st Airborne Division in September 1956.

During its seven years at Fort Campbell, the 11th Airborne Division made a significant and lasting physical and cultural impact. Shortly after its arrival in March 1949, the camp was redesignated a permanent Army fort, Fort Campbell, on 14 April 1950. The construction of permanent troop barracks, facilities and family housing began in 1950. As the first full-time division assigned to the city, the men of the 11th AD had the opportunity to name and memorialize many of these new facilities, roads and training areas, like the new airborne drop zones on the installation, after their heroes and their battlefields from their distinguished history in the World War II Pacific Theater of Operations and the Korean War. The major transition from a mobilization camp giant bachelor city to a modern national defense city began under the 11th Airborne Division.

As the 11th departed, the advance party of the soon-to-be-activated 101st Airborne Division (PENTOMIC) arrived, took up offices in T-39 and began transition planning. The famous World War II 101st Airborne Division had been inactivated in France in November 1945. A training division designated the 101st Training Division was activated at Camp Breckenridge, Kentucky (1948–53), and then transferred to Fort Jackson, South Carolina (1953–56). The soldiers of the 101st Training Division wore the Eagle shoulder patch of the 101st Airborne Division but did not wear the "airborne tab." They were basic trainees assigned to a training division for sixteen weeks; they were not airborne soldiers.

The new 101st Airborne Division (PENTOMIC) was to be a bold experiment to lift the Army out of its lowly status in the post–Korean War era and make it a fully modern, dynamic and relevant partner in the Cold War Defense Department. The new organization, equipment and doctrine of the PENTOMIC Army was the brainchild of the Army chief of staff, General Maxwell Taylor, who had been the World War II commander of the famous 101st Airborne Division. Because Fort Campbell was already undergoing modernization for a modern, married Army, because an airborne school had been built and because the training area had been modified to accommodate airborne training with drop zones for parachute operations, it was natural to select Fort Campbell as the home of an experimental airborne division. Because General Taylor had a deep personal attachment to the 101st Airborne, it was equally natural he would choose to reactivate that unit that was so much a part of his professional career for the experiment.

The new PENTOMIC organization was not based on the traditional divisional organization of three regiments (about 2,500 men per regiment and a total division personnel strength of 16,500) but on five lean airborne battle groups (about 600 men per battle group and a total division personnel strength of 11,500). These airborne battle groups could be spread widely across the modern battlefield to avoid becoming the tempting nuclear target that the old "two regiments up, one back" division presented. Modern FM and AM communications would keep the widely spread battle groups in contact. Above all, modern firepower would protect the widely spread battle groups. This new firepower included tactical nuclear missiles and mortars, the Honest John Rocket and the Davy Crocket nuclear mortar. Additionally, the new division was equipped so as to be fully air transportable; everything the division had could be put on Air Force transports. The new division trained to be ready for immediate deployment anywhere in the world in six hours. The combination of five airborne battle groups and a nuclear capability accounted for the designation PENTOMIC—five-sided (*penta*, Greek for five) and nuclear (*omic*, short for "atomic").[43]

To find enough airborne qualified soldiers to man the new 101st Airborne Division (PENTOMIC), the Army brought two of the old airborne regimental combat teams to Fort Campbell, the 187th ARTC and the 508th ARTC. The 187th had historic ties to the 11th Airborne Division. It had served in Korea (1950–53) and on occupation duty in Japan (1954–55) and was most recently assigned at Fort Bragg, North Carolina (1954–55), when it was transferred to Fort Campbell in 1956. The 508th ARTC had historic ties to the World War II 82nd Airborne Division. It was transferred from Fort Bragg to Fort Campbell in February 1954 and attached to the 11th Airborne Division. In June 1955, it was reorganized and sent to Japan to relieve the 187th ARTC on occupation duty in Japan. It returned to Fort Campbell in July 1956. The two ARTCs were inactivated in 1956, and the soldiers were transferred to the 101st Airborne Division. The soldiers from the six inactivated battalions were folded into the companies of the new airborne battle groups. The personnel transfer operation was nearly seamless.

The stationing of the 101st Airborne Division (PENTOMIC) at Fort Campbell heightened the already distinct airborne culture that the 11th Airborne Division had already begun. But more, the newness of the division and its promised capabilities now made the Army a part of the nuclear age. The modern Army and the modern, nuclear Air Force and Navy were represented on the fort together as the leading edge of the nation's defense. For its part, the 101st was designated as one of the Army's first-line divisions as part of the Army's new Strategic Army Corps (STRAC), reinforcing the requirement for the division to be able to deploy within six hours and reinforcing its elite status as a cutting-edge unit of the nation's offensive capabilities. Readiness tests and drills were part of the environment. Because of the strict recall requirements to meet the readiness requirements, leaves and passes for the airborne troopers were rare. In the days before cellphones and interstate highways, a trip to Nashville, for example, put one way outside the two-hour recall time that the division had established for itself. Consequently, a great reliance was put upon the Special Services Branch (the predecessor organization to

Top Three NCO Club circa 1955 on Ohio (Bastogne) near the present location of the Taylor Youth Center.

Morale, Welfare and Recreation, or MWR) to provide on-post recreation opportunities for soldiers and their families. Sports competitions, athletic teams, outdoor sports and especially the club system became needed outlets from the "Skilled, Tough, Ready to go Around the Clock" pressure that the STRAC environment induced.

CLARKSVILLE NAVAL BASE: 1948–1969

CAMPBELL AIR FORCE BASE: 1948–1959

What to do with the nuclear genie, now out of the bottle after Hiroshima and Nagasaki, was a crucial issue for Congress to sort out. The future development, testing, storage and control of nuclear weapons were thoroughly and passionately debated. The decision was that nuclear power was too critical to leave in the hands of either just the military sector or the civilian sector. The Atomic Energy Act of 1946 settled the issue. Congress divided control of atomic weapons between the civilian and military sectors. Responsibility for atomic energy was transferred from the wartime Manhattan Project to a new civilian-run organization called the Atomic Energy Commission (AEC). The AEC would later become the Department of Energy. The AEC was made responsible for the research, development, manufacture and delivery of atomic weapons and nuclear power. The military participation in the management of atomic weapons was exercised by a new joint command (meaning all branches of the military service contributed personnel and resources) called the Armed Forces Special Weapons Project (AFSWP). The AFSWP was made responsible for the storing, deploying, guarding, effects testing and training support for atomic weapons. The AFSWP is now called the Defense Atomic Support Agency.

Storage of the growing nuclear weapons stockpile was a first concern. Thirteen sites across the nation were carefully selected, and Camp Campbell was one of those locations. It was the second site chosen, and it was initially called Site Charlie. The reasons for choosing Camp Campbell as the location for Site Charlie were very nearly the same as those for choosing the area for a mobilization camp in July 1941. Many of those desirable features to support military operations were more fully developed as a result of the war years: the roads, the rail, the hospital, quartermaster support, etc. Especially important was the availability of an airfield. The small World War II Army air base, Campbell Army Air Base, located just north of the cantonment area, had been turned over the new Air Force as of 1948 and was renamed Campbell Air Force Base. During the years 1948 to 1959, one of the key missions of Campbell Air Force Base was to support the Strategic Air Command. The huge B-36 and B-52 bombers of the SAC could land at Campbell Air Force Base, load weapons from Site Charlie and continue on with their missions. When Site Charlie was activated, it became known as Clarksville Base.

It is a matter of curiosity as to which came first: Was it the Army's choice of Camp Campbell as the future home of the returning 11th Airborne Division that influenced the choice by the AEC of the location for Clarksville Base? Or could it have been the other way around, that the choice of Camp Campbell as the location of Clarksville Base by the AEC influenced the Army to move the 11th Airborne Division to Camp Campbell? These stationing decisions were made at about the same time. In the absence of any definitive evidence I have been able to find showing some kind of formal collaboration between the Army and the AEC, it is quite possible that each organization reached a

An aerial photograph of the 2,500-acre Clarksville Base located at the south end of the cantonment area along Mabry Road.

stationing decision independent of the other. What can be said, however, is that the practical results of the match between Clarksville Base and the 11th Airborne Division were most beneficial for the city of Fort Campbell.

The base was built for the AEC during 1947–48 by civilian contractors under the supervision of the Army Corps of Engineers. The base was five thousand acres large, or about three and a half square miles. It was located just to the west of the south end of the cantonment bounded by Mabry Road on the north. The main gate to the base was at Range Road (now called Market Garden Road) and Mabry Road. Range Road, two and a half miles long, connected the base directly with Campbell Air Force Base. The base was enclosed by four security fences; the third fence was electrified and protected by alarms and lights. The Little West Fork Creek passed through the base from west to east. At both ends, security bridges were installed featuring guard towers and roll-down overhead doors to seal off the creek access to intruders. Drainage and runoff culverts were equally made impenetrable to intruders. A spur from the Camp Campbell rail line was made to provide rail access into the base via special access through the four-fence barrier. In the coming years, special rail cars called Atomic Materials Rail Transport cars (ATMX) were built for the transport of nuclear weapons. The ATMX cars were a frequent sight.

Inside the base was a separately fenced-off administrative area (A-Area) and the larger portion of the base that was called the Q-Area. The A-Area was relatively small, about eight hundred acres. It provided generous space for the Navy and AEC headquarters and administrative support buildings. The A-Area contained the Marine barracks and all the facilities of a mini-camp. There was a chapel, swimming pool, gym, medical and dental clinic, officers' club and service club. Military personnel were also afforded full access to all the facilities on Fort Campbell for all other needs. No weapons work was conducted in the A-Area, but one needed a security clearance and special access to be there. The largest portion of the base, the Q-Area, was where the weapons were stored and worked on. "Q" came from the designation for the top-secret clearance compartmentalized program for

An artist's depiction of "Gravel Gertie."

nuclear weapons handling. One could not be in the Q-Area without a Q clearance badge. One would have to stop at a special guard post in the A-Area and trade his "A" clearance badge for his "Q" clearance badge before proceeding into the Q-Area and vice versa when coming out of the Q-Area. To be in the Q-Area without a Q clearance was to risk being shot by the Marine guards.

The buildings and facilities built inside this super secure base were designed to support nuclear operations. So unique were these buildings and facilities that Clarksville Base has been designated as eligible for the National Register of Historic Places because of its association with construction and storage of nuclear weapons in the early Cold War. It has been identified as a historic district and is itself a Cold War artifact. Of the thirteen bases, Clarksville Base is the only one that has been preserved. In 1969, the facilities at the base were turned over to and used by Fort Campbell and units assigned to Fort Campbell. The buildings were preserved by regular use and normal maintenance. The other twelve sites, unfortunately, were not useful or accessible to their tenant facilities, and those bases atrophied over time.

Some of the unusual architecture at Fort Campbell includes twenty-eight underground structures in which nuclear and nuclear-related material was stored. Eight of these underground structures had multiple chambers each protected by a Diebold bank vault door with two combination tumblers. This double tumbler feature enforced two-man/two-agency control of nuclear material. One combination was known by an AEC employee and the other by an AFSWP member. The feature served as a protection so that no one individual or no one agency could get control of a nuclear device. "Gravel Gerty," a pyramid-like building with a roof made of layers of gravel meant to contain radioactive material in the event of an accident, is a very unusual architectural artifact. Today, a large portion of the old base is open to the public. Information and maps for a self-guided driving tour are available through the Don F. Pratt Museum on Fort Campbell. Important sites are highlighted along the tour by explanatory signage.

The first AFSWP unit to occupy Clarksville Base was the Air Force 590th Aviation Squadron in August 1949. It was a special weapons assembly team. Special weapons teams, regardless of whether they were Army, Air Force or Navy, were capable of servicing any of the other military branch nuclear weapons. Navy technicians, for example, could easily service Air Force bombs—nuclear was nuclear. Responsibility for running and staffing the bases was divided between the military branches. From 1948 until 1952, the Air Force was responsible for Clarksville Base. Its proper name then was

Two vault doors inside an underground structure at Clarksville Base. Notice that each door has two combination dials. Two separate combinations were required to open each door protecting nuclear material.

Clarksville Air Force Base. In 1952, responsibility for the base was given to the Navy. A Navy captain commanded the base. Navy special weapons technicians performed the AFSWP functions. Marines provided the security. Because it was a Navy base, the name was changed to Clarksville Navy Base.

The Navy operated the base from 1952 until it was turned back to Fort Campbell in 1969. At the height of operations, there were about 550 Navy and Marine personnel assigned to the base.

The AEC maintained a staff to supervise the weapons and conduct quality assurance inspections and, later, weapons modification. Weapons and components were transported to the base, within the base and out of the base by the AEC weapons handlers. AEC staff also included positions called "operator," which was a weapons technician in support of the contractor's quality assurance and modification mission. The intensely scientific and quality assurance work was done for the AEC by a subcontractor, Sandia Laboratories. A second contractor, the civilian firm of Mason & Hanger-Silas Mason Company, Inc., was utilized by the AEC from 1960 to 1965 for weapons modification work. The AEC and contractor staff numbered between 160 and 230 personnel.

In addition to the AFSWP and AEC staff, Camp Campbell/Fort Campbell provided a small public works team for building, grass cutting and other routine facility maintenance. By an odd quirk of design, the Clarksville Base fence encompassed the sewage treatment/water reclamation plant for the entire Fort Campbell installation. The public works staff and those who

An early 1950s picture of the Atomic Energy Commission (AEC) weapons handlers at Clarksville Base.

worked at the sewage treatment plant, like everyone who worked inside the Q-Area, required a top-secret clearance to be in a facility that housed nuclear weapons. To treat sewage at Fort Campbell during the Cold War required a top-secret clearance!

The World War II Campbell Army Air Base was turned over to the newly created Air Force in late 1947. The Air Force allocated the base the Strategic Air Command on 1 July 1948. The 4002nd Base Service Squadron was the first Air Force unit assigned to the SAC base. A base service squadron did not have aircraft. Its mission was to run the operations at an airfield: the control tower, flight operations, refueling, weather and crash and rescue. Many aircraft operations were conducted out of the air base. There were hundreds of takeoffs and landings each month. Many were troop airlift operations in support of Army airborne training at Fort Campbell. The air base averaged between 400 and 600 flights per month. A good portion of the operations, on average about 125 per month, were in support of SAC. Some of those SAC missions were training missions, and some were operational missions. Nuclear weapons were transported to and from the air base by AEC weapons handlers who were escorted by extremely tight Marine Corps security. Some of the missions were training missions to familiarize SAC aircraft crews with procedures. Some of the missions were for the transporting of weapons from and to overseas nuclear storage areas, and some, I suspect, were "deception missions" deliberately undertaken with false cargo to confuse Soviet intelligence about the real numbers and locations of active nuclear weapons around the world.

Campbell Air Force Base was turned back to the Army and Fort Campbell on 1 January 1959. It was renamed Campbell Army Airfield. The Air Force continued to support the airfield with air base support operations. SAC flights and operations with Clarksville Base continued as before, as well as all other Air Force operations, including troop airlift support of airborne operations.

Secrecy about what took place at the base was a way of life for all who worked there. The base was blacked out on military topographical maps and was a designated no fly-over zone by the FAA. The existence and location of the base, however, was not a secret. It was plain to be seen by anyone who drove by. Over 160 AEC civilians lived in the Hopkinsville-Clarksville area. Marines and Navy personnel frequented the towns. Everyone knew something important and something nuclear went on within those four security fences. Because of the fences and the secrecy, the silence of those who worked there and the mystique of the whole nuclear program, the base took on the nickname "the Birdcage" or sometimes even "the Squirrel Cage."

An artist's depiction of the four security fences that surrounded Clarksville Base.

The Navy and Air Force personnel and families assigned to the base integrated fully into the life of the city of Fort Campbell. Many spouses worked on post. Children attended the post schools and participated in youth sports teams and activities. Though Clarksville Base had its own chapel, some chose services held outside the fence and became part of those denominational communities. The post newspaper, the *Courier*, which began publication in 1950, carried in its social pages all the news of the Clarksville Base Officers' Wives Club. The post telephone book provided a virtual organizational chart of the workings of Clarksville Base and the Air Force base, as well as the name, rank and address of all Navy and Air Force personnel living on post.

The transition of the giant bachelor city to a national defense city very much included the need for permanent troop quarters and family housing. Both the Air Force and the Navy contributed to those efforts. The Navy built a brick troop barracks for the unmarried Marine and Navy enlisted personnel and a seventy-unit housing area in the near vicinity of the base called Clarksville Base Annex. The street names in the Navy housing area were distinctly Navy: Forrestal, Halsey and Byrd in honor of famous admirals and O'Bannon in honor of the Marine Corps hero of the battle in Tripoli against the Barbary pirates. An athletic field in the housing area was memorialized in honor of Patrick Carmody, a nuclear weapons technician who died at sea aboard the nuclear submarine USS *Thresher*. The Marine barracks became home to the men of the 2-17th Cavalry Squadron of the 101st Airborne Division on their return from Vietnam in 1972. It is now the location of the division's Noncommissioned Officer Academy. Clarksville Base Annex was absorbed into the post housing inventory in 1969 and renamed Gardner Hills. The street names were changed to honor Army soldiers. The Air Force also built a small family housing area near the air base on Glider Road. It was called Hedgerow Court. Four permanent 160-man dormitories, as the Air Force calls its barracks, were built on the airfield. The Air Force dormitories still stand. They were upgraded several times, most recently to meet modern troop housing guidelines. They are now used for Army single-soldier housing. The old family quarters at Hedgerow Court were recently upgraded and modified for use as office space for the American Red Cross, Army Emergency Relief and other agencies. The Air Force no longer has a requirement to provide family housing on Fort Campbell. Air Force families are eligible and integrated into family housing.

PERMANENT BARRACKS AND THE DOUBLE CHEVRON PLAN: 1948–1962

When the 11th Airborne Division arrived at Camp Campbell in March 1949, the headquarters moved into T-39 and the soldiers moved into the temporary mobilization barracks of the World War II camp. The buildings, roads and facilities were in poor condition. Family housing—what little of it there was—was in a dismal state also. The postwar family housing stock consisted of 15 prewar farmhouses, 14 apartments in the Station Hospital and 732 sets of family quarters made by modifying open-bay Series 800 barracks into four-plex apartments. The first action to be taken was the very pressing need to address permanent troop housing. The challenge of fixing the troop housing could be done in-house, meaning that the Army could use Major Construction Army (MCA) funds to plan and build. Funding, construction and administration of permanent family housing would prove more problematic.

Fortunately, in anticipation of the arrival of the 11th Airborne Division and the probable upgrading of the temporary camp to a permanent fort, the post engineer had developed a master plan to address future development. The 1948 Master Plan was the first attempt to organize the postwar cantonment and set the tone for future development of the post. The purpose of the 1948 Master Plan was to guide long-range construction plans and budgets for modern permanent facilities and structures. The 1948 plan assumed troop strength of one division, fifteen thousand personnel. The master plan would be amended, however, in 1951 and again in 1953 concerning the probable number of soldiers to be assigned to the newly designated fort. The number was amended upward in 1951 to thirty thousand soldiers, or planning for the stationing of two divisions. The number was amended downward in 1953 to seventeen thousand, or the stationing of one division. The up and down assumption of troop numbers was likely the result of strategic assessment to expand the Army in 1950 followed by a reappraisal to downsize the Army in 1953 because of President Eisenhower's "New Look" and his reliance on a smaller conventional force bolstered by a bigger nuclear deterrence strategy.

As with the World War II Series 800 Plan of 1942, the Army developed a standard construction plan for the new and modern permanent barracks in 1949. The standard building plan was a three-story brick structure designed to provide orderly rooms, offices and day rooms on the first floor; house 225 soldiers on the second and third floors; and provide a company arms room and supply room in the basement level. Each had an attached company mess hall. The old six-building requirement for a company-size unit area in the Series 800 plan was reduced to one all-inclusive, permanent building in the new plan. The building looked like a hammer when seen from above, with the three stories of offices and living space making the appearance of the long handle of the hammer and the one-story mess hall perpendicular to the main building looking proportionally like the hammerhead. The proper name was Permanent Troop Housing and Supporting Facility; the nickname was hammerhead. The first construction of this design for the Army was at Fort Campbell. Construction began in June 1951. Fifty-seven hammerheads were built from 1951 to 1953. This provided enough troop housing for 12,825 soldiers. The total availability of the modern permanent housing was, however, less than the total strength of the 11th and definitely less than the total fort soldier population that included tenant units and the garrison soldiers. A shortage of permanent troop housing and

New permanent cinder block construction troop housing nicknamed "hammerheads" for the hammer-like appearance as seen from above. The three-story troop building represented the handle, and the one-story mess hall on the end represented the hammer.

administrative office space has been a perennial problem at Fort Campbell ever since. A great reliance, therefore, was placed on the stock of World War II mobilization structures to make up the difference. Even in 2014, seventy-two years later, some of the World War II stock is still in service for office, maintenance and warehouse use. Initial appropriations in 1950–51 to build the permanent facilities construction was augmented by separate appropriations of $620,000 for the upgrade and modernization of twenty blocks of the World War II stock.

Where to build the new troop housing was a serious planning issue. It was not feasible to tear down some of the World War II stock and build new structures on top of where it had been. The existing water, sewage, electrical and road infrastructure would not have been easily compatible with the new building. New ground was preferable, and it was available. The choicest ground lay between the western boundary of the old cantonment, Kansas Avenue (Desert Storm Avenue), and Range Road (Market Garden Road). A small rise in elevation running north–south between the proposed building site and Range Road nicely separated the troop area from the small arms ranges.

The spine of the old camp troop housing ran north–south from 1st Street to 59th Street between Tennessee and Indiana Avenues. The spine of the new

Permanent troop housing being built in the early 1950s. The building on the right is 3211 at the intersection of Indiana Avenue and 42nd Street looking south.

permanent troop housing was planned to parallel the old spine by running north–south from 11th Street to 56th Street between Colorado Avenue (the road is now gone, but it is very roughly defined by a new road, New Market Road) and Kansas Avenue (now Desert Storm Avenue). Kansas Avenue became the "Main Street" of the new troop housing area because it ran the length of the line. The area was often called the "troop line." Much of the new construction planned through the 1950s (pools, gyms, clinics, a football and baseball stadium, a central chapel, service clubs, a movie theater, etc.) was built along this avenue. Four new motor pool facilities were built parallel to the troop line west of Colorado Avenue. The Airborne School was built within a six-square-block area along the troop line between 18th (Air Assault Street) to the south, 21st Street on the north, Kansas Avenue on the east and Colorado on the west. By the early 1960s, the troop line along Kansas was a very modern and very nearly self-contained troop living area providing all essential on- and off-duty resources within walking distance of each airborne battle group.

Forty-nine of the new hammerheads were built along the troop line. On a map or site plan, the neat rows of buildings gave the appearance of a chevron on the right sleeve of a uniform jacket. The imagery of a chevron worked well when, in 1951, the master plan was amended to accommodate troop housing for a second division. On paper, a second troop line was planned on the opposite, or east, side of the old World War II spine. This second troop line would have been bound by Kentucky Avenue on the west and Indiana Avenue on the east. The two-division plan came to be called the "Double Chevron Plan." It was never executed because, in 1953, the master plan was again amended based on new guidance for reduced troop strength down to seventeen thousand soldiers, or just one division. To get an appreciation of

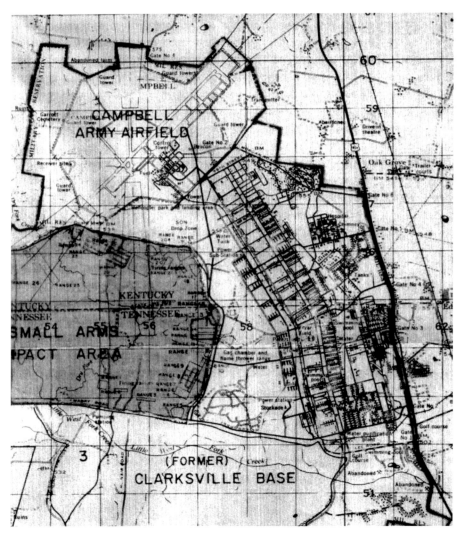

A 1973 map showing the relationship between Clarksville Base, the cantonment area and Campbell Army Airfield (former Campbell Air Force Base).

what the Double Chevron may have looked like, one can see on the map the eight hammerheads that were built between Kentucky Avenue and Indiana Avenue and 42nd Street to 46th Street. Imagine the addition of forty more hammerheads stretching forty more blocks north and south along Indiana Avenue. The eight hammerheads built between Kentucky and Indiana Avenues were not the start of a Double Chevron plan. They were, in fact, the first of the forty-nine hammerheads built. In the 1950s and '60s, they housed the 937th Engineer Group, a 2nd Army tenant unit that was not part of the 11th Airborne Division.

Temporary Family Housing Solutions: Farmhouses, "Splinter Village," the Hospital and a Trailer Park

With permanent troop housing underway, the continuing challenge was that of family housing. The great citizen Army of World War II could not have been, should not have been and was not a married Army. It was raised for a single purpose: to win the war and, when won, to beat its swords back into plow shares. But the prewar Regular Army did have a tradition of providing housing for career married soldiers. A career soldier was defined as a corporal with seven years' time or more in service. The new Army of the Cold War was seven times larger than the pre–World War II Regular Army. It was fast becoming a hybrid organization made of the old Regular Army and a new full-time version of the citizen Army of World War II. It faced the challenge and the necessity of providing family housing but now for a much larger organization on forts that had only recently been mobilization camps. Hence, as Camp Campbell made the postwar transition to a permanent fort, it began with a rather dismal collection of some old farmhouses, converted barracks and apartments at the Station Hospital.

The "dismal collection" of available family housing does have an important place in the history of housing on Fort Campbell. Though it might have been dismal, it was an important attempt to make the best use of local resources to solve a very critical problem. Among the fifteen old farmhouses were the four historic homes mentioned in Chapter 2. Three of those homes became general officer quarters and are still in use today. One served for a time as the quarters for the command sergeant major and then as the offices for the Cultural Resources Branch of the Department

The first family government housing on post after World War II. Series 800 barracks in the vicinity of what is now Stryker Village were converted into four-plex apartments. The nickname for this temporary housing area was "Splinter Village."

of Public Works. The other homes—not nearly as nice as the four special homes—were in use through the 1950s, but eventually they came down due to excessive maintenance costs.

The largest amount of early enlisted family housing came from the conversion of several blocks of World War II barracks into a housing area of four-plex apartments. The area was located between Gates 3 and 4 along Fort Campbell Boulevard (U.S. Highway 41A). The project was undertaken by Fort Campbell, managed by Fort Campbell and maintained with Army money. It was government housing. This housing area was located in the place of the current Stryker Village Housing Area. Because the housing was made from old barracks and slightly on the rustic side, the area took on the nickname "Splinter Village."

Modifications to the old barracks provided for four comfortable two-bedroom apartments per building. Each apartment had a kitchen, bath, dining room and large living room. Each family had a separate entrance, but all four families shared a common coal-fired boiler. Coal soot was a problem in the winter, and agreement about the single thermostat setting was a matter of daily negotiation. The blocks of buildings were laid out in military order, but landscaping, a few swing sets and a basketball hoop or

Children were not allowed in the commissary during the 1950s. A nursery was located next to the commissary to care for children so Army mothers could shop.

two helped to provide a more neighborhood-like feeling over time. A row of single-story buildings of the type that had served as orderly rooms and mess halls stretched along Virginia Avenue between Gates 3 and 4. One of those buildings was the old World War II commissary, the first and original camp commissary. The Virginia Street building served as the post commissary until November 1956. The 1956–78 commissary was located near Splinter Village, just across the Gate 3 access road, Jackson Street (Air Assault Boulevard), on Florida Avenue, Building 832. The second commissary on post was a fourteen-year-old World War II warehouse modified and updated to become a modern shopping facility. The post's first gas station was located across the street from the commissary. Building 832 is still in use, but it is now the home of the Command Visual Information Center and the post television studios.

The buildings adjacent to the Virginia Street commissary were modified for a variety of family-centered activities. The building next to the commissary became a child-care nursery, a feature that was made necessary as children were not allowed in the commissary. For that matter, neither were women in hair curlers, shorts or pants. There was a strict dress code and rules of conduct at the commissary. Buildings for use as Boy and Girl

Scout meeting centers were made available. While far from ideal, one can see in the Splinter Village community the outline of a modern Army family housing community with its neighborhood appearance, community center buildings and services and proximity to convenient shopping. One is tempted to think that if only Starbucks, Inc., had been in business at the time it would have been, on paper at least, a nearly a perfect housing area prototype for the future.

A third part of the early family housing stock was the use of fourteen apartments in the Station Hospital for enlisted family housing. The Station Hospital was a huge brick veneer complex of forty-six interconnected wards capable of providing beds for 2,134 patients. The hospital was scaled back after World War II but was ramped up again in the early part of the Korean War (1951) to 1,350 beds. By 1953, it was downsized to 300 beds. As the hospital consolidated its operations into less space, it made for thousands of extra square feet of space. The extra space was used clear through the

An aerial view of the old Station Hospital complex from the south looking north toward the airfield. The Sunday school class can be seen forming a human cross outside the hospital chapel.

1990s for many purposes, including extra classrooms for the schools, a post guardhouse, the post nursery, the thrift shop, a location for chaplain's activities, an Officers' Club Annex, a barbershop and for a time as the home of the Noncommissioned Officers' Academy. One of the biggest uses of the extra space, however, was dedicated to transient family housing. Transient housing was a temporary hotel-like facility provided for incoming and outgoing families. Several of the large wards on the southwest side of the complex were modified for this use.

A new hospital (Blanchfield) was built in 1982. A new transient housing facility (George Turner) was built in 1997. Almost all of the old hospital came down by 2001; only three of the forty-seven original wards survived. They are all that remain of the once large hospital complex. The three former wards serve today as office space for the provost marshal and the staff judge advocate general. They are located on Forrest Road. By a sweet coincidence, those three wards once served as the OB-GYN clinic of the hospital. They stand as if in honor of the birthplace of many Fort Campbell

Housing could not be built fast enough to meet demand. A trailer park area was established on post near 54th and Indiana Avenue to provide additional enlisted housing.

Army brat baby boomers and Army children of the Vietnam era. The space on which the old Station Hospital complex once stood is now vacant. The perimeter roads are still in place. Future plans are for the site to be used for the newest and most contemporary family housing on the post.

A fourth type of housing was offered as a temporary and local fix to the family housing shortage: a trailer park. It offered 129 spaces. It was located on Indiana Avenue at 56th Street. For a time, surplus government trailers were offered for rent for those who could not afford their own. Mention of the availability of a trailer park for housing and pictures of the facility never appeared in welcome and newcomer guidebooks, except for one year, 1968, which even included a picture. One gets the impression that the fort chose not to highlight the trailer park as an example of how the Army takes care of its families. The trailer park faded out of the inventory in the early 1970s. Where it was located is now the home of the second brigade combat team soldier housing area constructed in the early 1980s.

A PRIVATE SECTOR SOLUTION TO THE SHORTAGE OF FAMILY HOUSING: WHERRY AND CAPEHART HOUSING, 1949–1962

The truth of the matter was that after ten years of the Great Depression (1930–40) and four years of world war (1941–45), the entire nation faced a housing crisis. Young men and women who had faced the deprivation and separation of the war years were more than ready for what was to become the baby boom of the 1950s. The nation was in a scramble to solve the housing shortage, and so were the armed forces. Secretary of Defense Louis A. Johnson recognized the magnitude of the problem as it applied to attracting young men and women to the armed forces and defined it as a matter of national security:

> *Rather than be separated from their families because of lack of Government quarters and scarcity of rental housing at their places of assignment, many of the service personnel have accepted disgraceful living conditions in shacks, trailer camps and overcrowded buildings, many at extortionate rents. It cannot be expected that competent individuals will long endure such conditions... There is nothing more vital or pressing in the interest of morale and the security of America than proper housing for our Armed Forces.*[44]

The crux of the problem was how to finance the expansion of permanent family housing. Neither Congress nor the president was forthcoming with appropriated funds for solving the family housing crisis. It was too expensive a line item to add to the Defense Department budget. If not by an outright appropriation, then the solution would be to attract private sector developers to finance, build, maintain and operate affordable rental housing on or near military installations. The scheme depended on private companies investing a large amount of money in building a subdivision and then making their return and profit in the form of rents collected over time.

The challenge interested financiers faced was risk. First, they needed the assurance that the installation would not be closed or that the number of soldiers would not fluctuate down. Their return on investment depended on a nearly full occupancy rate. Second, a private sector investment like this depended on mortgage insurance that would protect the developer from undue risk in the event that the project failed through no fault of its own. To mitigate risk and attract investors, federal law (the National Housing Act of 1934) needed to be amended. The Wherry Act, which added Title VIII to the existing National Housing Act, made the needed changes to protect the financiers. It was signed into law by President Truman on 8 August 1949.

Senator Kenneth S. Wherry (R, NE), self-admittedly not a real estate or finance expert, proposed the solution. The first generation of post–World War II Army family housing still bears his name, "Wherry Housing." The name does not refer to the developer, style, design or type of housing but only to the way it was financed. Housing areas that were financed by the Wherry program, however, were often called the "Wherry Housing Area," and Wherry Housing tended to be smaller, less attractive and more austere than later housing. Wherry Housing on one installation did not necessarily look like Wherry Housing on another. Developers from installation to installation took designs off the shelf from a multitude of housing plans being developed for the rapidly expanding postwar subdivision market.

The Wherry Act provided that the secretary of defense would establish and administer a Military Housing Insurance Fund (MHIF), lease land for the potential housing areas on military installations for a nominal fee and sell to the developer needed utilities (water, sewage, disposal, electrical and telephone). The developer (sponsor) would finance, build, operate and maintain the housing project. The Corps of Engineers would supervise the construction, and the Federal Housing Authority (FHA) would ensure federal guidelines for design and livability were met. Wherry Housing was not government quarters. It was a private housing project operating on

Wherry Housing, the first Lee Village.

post in order to provide rental property to Army families. It had an office within the housing area. Soldiers received their Basic Allowance for Quarters (BAQ), entered a rental agreement and paid their rent to the provider as they would have in any other private rental agreement. The rent did not necessarily reflect BAQ, but the rental price established by the developer was to meet his mortgage requirement and a 4 percent profit margin per unit.

The 11th Airborne Division and post commander, Major General William Miley, was quick to take advantage of the program when it became law. He made a request for 400 units just three months after the passage of the bill, in November 1949. Two more increments of 400 units were made. By 1952, there were 1,200 units of Wherry Housing built on the installation. The Midwest Mortgage Company of Louisville, Kentucky, provided the financing, and the construction and management was done by two of its subsidiary companies, American Homes and Dixie Homes. Sixty-five unused and undeveloped acres in the northeast of the cantonment were leased for the purpose. The construction design was a four- to eight-plex brick town house design. The design was comparable with contemporary rental apartments for the time. The Wherry Housing Area was known by that name until it was renamed Lee Village in honor of the first commander of the 101ˢᵗ Airborne Division, Major General William E. Lee, in October 1959. Lee Village was the only Wherry project built at Fort Campbell. With available temporary government quarters (Splinter Village, etc.) and the new Wherry Housing, the stock of family housing in 1953 went up to 2,000 units. The original Lee Village served as enlisted housing until it was demolished and replaced by modern town houses in two increments. In 2006–7, 440 units came down, and the remaining units came down in 2010.[45]

In early 1954, the Wherry program came under intense congressional scrutiny. It was alleged that unscrupulous builders aided by corrupt FHA officials were reaping huge windfall profits at the expense of the taxpayer. There were no allegations of misconduct at Fort Campbell, but the program began to wind down and was replaced by a second privatization program. The new follow-on program was named the Capehart Program after its sponsor, Senator Homer E. Capehart (R, ID). The Capehart Program legislation became law on 11 August 1955.

Capehart Housing, like Wherry before it, referred to the method of financing, not the style, but changes in the program did allow for homes of larger specification and a movement away from multi-unit town houses toward more single-family and duplex-style housing. At Fort Campbell, most of the Capehart Housing (1955–62) was single-level, duplex, Ranch style easily distinguishable from Wherry Housing, and the Ranch style made it so readily identifiable as Capehart Housing that the program name and the Ranch style become one in the minds of most.

An important distinction between Wherry and Capehart Program housing was that while both were financed and built by private developers, once built, Capehart Housing came under military control. Fort Campbell administered and maintained Capehart Housing, and it truly became government housing. The Wherry Program was phased out from 1955 to 1959. The Wherry investors were bought out at fair market value by the Army, and Lee Village was absorbed into the government housing stock.

Fort Campbell moved quickly on the new Capehart Program. Authorization and a contract with the Clark Construction Company of Owensboro, Kentucky, were approved, and a groundbreaking ceremony to celebrate the start of construction was held on 15 August 1955. The ceremony was attended by Tennessee senator Albert Gore Sr. It was held at the corner of Forrest and Reed Roads, the site of the NCO quarters portion of the project.

The project was to build 223 units of NCO quarters, 64 units of company-grade officer quarters and 19 units of senior officer quarters. The three

The Wherry PX located near the Wherry Housing area (Lee Village).

housing areas were initially named, unimaginatively, the NCO area, the company-grade area and the senior-grade area. The reason for the naming delay was that construction overlapped the departure of the 11th Airborne Division and the arrival of the 101st Airborne Division. The 101st Airborne Division Memorialization Committee conferred names on the NCO and senior-grade areas on 6 January 1959. The NCO area was named Hammond Heights in honor of Corporal Lester Hammond Jr., a Medal of Honor recipient who had earned the award while serving with the 187th ARTC in Korea. The inactivated 187th ARTC had been absorbed as part of the new 101st Airborne Division (PENTOMIC). The division included the 1-187th Airborne Battle Group. The senior-grade housing area was named in honor of Lieutenant Colonel William L. Turner, commander of the 1-506th PIR, 101st Airborne Division, in Normandy and awarded the Distinguished Service Cross (DSC). The company-grade housing area was not dedicated until June 1961. It was named in honor of Captain Fred O. Drennen, 502nd PIR, 101st Airborne Division, who was awarded the DSC for action near Best, Holland, in September 1944.

The last of the Capehart Program Housing Areas was named Stryker Village. It was built on the site of Splinter Village from 1962 to 1964. It provided modern duplex housing for enlisted soldiers and was named in honor of Medal of Honor recipient Private First Class Paul Stryker, 513th PIR, 17th Airborne Division. Stryker Village and the last of the expansions in the existing housing areas got in under the wire of Capehart funding. Like the Wherry Program before it, the Capehart Program came under intense congressional scrutiny for fraud, waste and abuse. The Senate voted to end private funding in favor of direct appropriations. Negotiations with the House allowed for an extension of the program to finish projects underway. No new housing construction would take place in the city until the 1970s, when the 101st Airborne Division returned from Vietnam in April 1972.[46]

Over the 1950s and into the early 1960s, a pattern developed in the layout of the city. The troop line of permanent soldier housing and all the relevant amenities for single soldiers developed west of the old spine of the original cantonment. All the housing areas developed east of the old spine parallel to U.S. 41A. Housing tended to a pattern of lower enlisted housing in the north (Lee Village), NCO in the middle (Hammond Heights) and officer housing in the south (Drennen Park, Turner Loop and Cole Park). The officer club and its facilities were located in the south near Gate 1, where the vast majority of officer housing was located. The exceptions to the pattern were Stryker Village and four buildings of bachelor officer quarters providing sixty-four sets of apartments located at Tennessee and 41st Street, a long three miles from the officers' club facilities.

Schools, Clubs and Army Society in the National Defense City

A giant bachelor city did not need schools for children. Those who brought families to Camp Campbell in World War II resided off post, and their children attended local public or parochial schools. But when the city began its transformation to a national defense city with Army families and the beginnings of Army housing, the need for schools naturally followed. It was a need that was initially met by transporting Camp Campbell children twelve miles by military bus to attend Clarksville Public Schools. In 1947, the Clarksville School Board organized a K–3 school on the camp. The classrooms were scattered in separate buildings in the temporary government housing like Splinter Village.

The cost of absorbing children in the local school district or of providing classroom instruction on post was substantial. School districts are funded by local property taxes. Camp Campbell families were not assessed local property tax and were technically not paying their way for schooling. The problem of economic and infrastructure stress placed on communities adjacent to military bases had been addressed in World War II by the Latham Act, a means of providing federal subsidies to local communities for services. Recognizing that local communities would continue to be pressed by needs generated by postwar military bases, Congress passed Public Law 814 in 1950. The law provided funding for the construction and maintenance of schools on federal land where needed.[47]

Shortly after passage of Public Law 814, Major General Lyman Lemitzer, commander of the 11th Airborne Division and Fort Campbell, appointed a school board. The board hired a superintendent and was ready to open the city's first school in 1951. The school was located in Building 126 of the Station Hospital, a two-story brick veneer building. Twenty-four classroom teachers and three special education teachers were hired. Junior and senior high school students continued to attend Clarksville schools. The Clarksville School District received reimbursements for Fort Campbell students who attended its schools.

The first Fort Campbell School built with Public Law 814 funding was built in the new Wherry Housing Area. It was a wonderfully modern facility with twenty-five classrooms, a gym, a cafeteria, music rooms and a school nurse's office. We know it today as Lincoln School, but from 1952 to 1960, it was called the Wherry Elementary School. It offered grades K through 6.

The Wherry School was built two years before the landmark 1954 *Brown v. Topeka Board of Education* Supreme Court decision that overturned the old doctrine of "separate but equal is equal." Like the Army since the overturn

Wherry School (Lincoln Elementary School), the first on-post school. Wherry Housing area (Lee Village) can be seen in the background.

of segregation in 1948, and like the Wherry Housing Area itself, Wherry Elementary was racially integrated. Clarksville and Hopkinsville schools remained racially segregated into the early 1960s. Wherry Elementary School was much ahead of its time. In 1952, it stood out as a model in a region that was still deeply infected with Jim Crow segregation.

Wherry was expanded in October 1955 and again in 1957. The expansion buildings were called the Wherry School Annex. It provided additional space for kindergarten classes, two additional sixth-grade classrooms and an overflow for home economics classes for the junior high school. Wherry School Annex expanded enough to become its own school and was renamed Barkley School in 1960.

The growth of the Fort Campbell School System followed the growth and development of the family housing system. Officer housing was being built in Drennen Park, Turner Loop and Cole Park a distant three miles away from Wherry Elementary. To fill the need for a neighborhood school in the south end of the city, a K–6 school was established in temporary buildings, Buildings 1470 and 1472, near 1st and Alaska Avenues. It was named South School. South School operated as a K–6 school until 1958, when Jackson School was opened at 11th and Mississippi Avenues. South School continued

The newly built (1965) Fort Campbell High School, now the Mahaffey Middle School. Stryker Village is in the background.

The Fort Campbell High School cheerleaders, 1961.

to provide classroom space for overcrowded sixth and seventh graders until Marshall Elementary School was built in 1962.

In 1957, a separate junior high school was built for grades seven through nine. The building also served as the senior high school until a permanent one was built in 1965. The junior high school building was located on Forrest Road, just south of the Station Hospital. It was renamed Wassom Middle School in honor of Brigadier General Herbert M. Wassom on 9 June 1989. The high school built in 1965 served as such until 1985. When the new high school was built in 1985, the old high school became the current Mahaffey Middle School.

Off-duty and Army family social life evolved and grew with the city during the 1950s transition. Fort Campbell in the 1950s and early 1960s remained fairly remote from Hopkinsville and Clarksville. Many who were children during that era recall that one could ride a bike as far south as Ringgold Creek (seven miles) before encountering any serious building along Fort Campbell Boulevard. The distance from the towns made for a sort of isolation wherein the growing Army community became self-sufficient. With housing and schools, Fort Campbell became more and more like a real city, and a city unto itself.

There were several traditional organizations of the prewar Regular Army and from the giant bachelor city of the war years that were easily adaptable to the new Army and national defense city. The chapel system, the officer and noncommissioned officer open mess system and the Special Services Branch were ready-made to be of service to Army families. What would be new would be a demand for youth services and activities. That void was filled by a unique organization called the Dad's Club.

Adapting the chapel system to include family activities was not difficult. It was estimated in 1965 that 30 percent of the post population attended church services. There had been fourteen chapels, all stretched along the length of Indiana Avenue, during the war. The chapels were small and lacked space for gatherings and programs. Additional space for religious activities was made available at the spacious Station Hospital. Bible studies, religious instruction, Sunday school and Catechism classes were easily accommodated. A new central chapel, Soldiers Chapel, was built in the center of the troop line with much additional space for chapel activities. A robust staff of twenty-five chaplains saw to the needs of soldiers and families of all denominations.[48]

The club system easily transitioned from the bachelor years to a new mission of service to Army families. The officer and the NCO open mess systems were governed by Army Regulations 210-50 and 210-60. The regulations allowed that each club system was under the control of the local commander and was self-supporting. The post commander exercised a great deal of influence over how his club system operated. A board of governors was elected from the membership annually to conduct all business of the club. The commander could appoint an advisory council. Membership fees and dues were assessed. Membership was voluntary, but under the unspoken rules of Army tradition, it was expected.[49]

A new Officers' Club was built in 1963. It replaced a wooden World War II facility that had been located near the center of the post. The new building was built near the officer housing areas that were located in the south of the cantonment near Gate 1. The building was plush and cost over $700,000. It provided a ballroom and dining room that could accommodate three hundred. There were a cocktail lounge, casual bar, TV room, reading room, beauty parlor and barbershop. Outside were a swimming pool and tennis courts. Nearby were the golf club and Cole Park picnic area. Operated by the officers of the post in their own interest, family accommodations were a natural fit. When the club system faltered in the late 1990s and transitioned to a community club system, the Officers' Club was converted to the present Family Readiness facility.

The NCO open mess system operated thirteen branches across the post. The main NCO club, the Top Five Club, was built at a cost of nearly $1 million in 1964. It was a posh and trendy building featuring two exotic dining rooms in the round. While the Top Five was clearly the central NCO club, the NCO system also operated a Top Three Club; eleven other NCO clubs spread across the post from the Campbell Army Airfield to the outdoor recreation facilities developing south of the cantonment along Woodland Drive; the Rod and Gun Club; the riding stables; and the Lake Taal recreation area. The old Top Five Club was located in the center of the city at the corner of Normandy Drive (25th Street) and Kentucky Avenue across from the Dryer Field House and next to Boldando Pool. It is now the DEERS/ID and Human Resources Directorate Building. The USO also shares part of the old Top Five Club.

The club system provided much-needed social contact, rest and relaxation for the soldiers and families of the high-pressure STRAC 101st Airborne Division. The club system also provided the foundation and resources for the Officers' Wives Club and the NCO Wives Club. The NCO Wives called their organization the Zebra Club (for the sergeant's stripes on their husbands' uniforms). The wives clubs provided a special embodiment of Army tradition and culture. It was in these clubs that Army tradition was promoted and new wives and families were acculturated into

The swank and trendy Top Five Main NCO Club.

the larger Army family. "White gloves and party manners" describes well the culture of that different era of the national defense city, a culture that is sometimes today called "Old Army."

The Special Services Branch (SSB) was organized in 1942 under the Army Service Forces. Its mission was to stimulate, develop and maintain the physical well-being of military personnel through participation in a planned recreational and morale program. Officers and enlisted members of the SSB coached sports teams, checked out equipment, maintained gyms and athletic fields and coordinated entertainment. A robust sports program was very much a part of the giant bachelor city, but the emphasis on competitive sports only continued to grow in the 1950s. Post teams competed against other post teams, local colleges and even semi-pro teams. Fryar Football Stadium and Perez Baseball Field, built in 1959, were first-class stadiums and the sites of quality sporting events.

SSB also employed a good number of civilians. Civilian members wore a SSB uniform. For women, this was a gray suit with a distinctive shoulder patch. The women operated the enlisted service clubs, which operated outside the officer and NCO open mess system. There were four service clubs. SSB also operated the libraries and craft centers and coordinated soldier entertainment. The SSB played an important role in helping to establish and run outdoor recreation facilities. These new outdoor facilities were developed in the early 1950s especially in the favorable terrain south of the cantonment along Woodlawn Road. A recreation area was developed around Lake Taal, a rod and gun club was staffed to support sport shooting and hunting on post and a horse stable was built to support riding and boarding. By 1965, organization of the SSB was becoming increasingly civilian-led. For the first time in its history at Fort Campbell, civilian directors of the sports, service clubs, library, crafts and entertainment branch were hired.[50]

New to the married Army was the need to provide activities for youth at a level beyond what could be provided by the open mess system or the SSB. A Youth Activities Center (YAC) was established. Its mission was to sponsor activities, wholesome recreation and entertainment that would contribute to the happiness and general well-being of the youth of the post. The YAC at Fort Campbell was named the Dad's Club. A parents' committee with representation from each housing area provided for active parent participation and oversight. A good many of the programs, Scouting, Little League, cheerleading, dances and other activities were staffed and led by interested and involved parents, as was the case in any other American community of the time. The Dad's Club did have a facility from which to operate located on Polk Road between the

The Rod and Gun Club, outdoor recreation.

Lee Village and Hammond Heights Housing Areas. In many ways, the Dad's Club exemplified the finishing and appropriate touch to the development of an Army national defense city culture that supported the needs of the Army family of the early Cold War.[51]

Something new was afoot in the national defense city of the early 1960s. The nature of the Cold War was changing. A new president had been elected. John F. Kennedy had run on a campaign program called the "New Frontier." The Soviet Union was pursuing a program of supporting "wars of national liberation." One of those efforts appeared to be occurring in a faraway place called the Republic of South Vietnam. A large advisory effort up to sixteen thousand soldiers was underway. Not units but individual officers and soldiers were assigned to the Military Assistance Command–Vietnam (MACV). Many of these advisors were assigned to Fort Campbell on their return. The *Fort Campbell Courier* carried many articles about the presentation of medals for meritorious service and gallantry in action as awards followed the advisors home.

With the New Frontier came a commitment to meet the new Soviet challenge toe to toe, "to pay any price," as the president promised

The new (1965) Main Exchange, now called the Mini-Mall. Behind the exchange, where the wooden barracks are in the photograph, is where the new division headquarters building stands today.

in his inaugural address. The Peace Corps and the new Green Beret were means to meet that challenge at the lower end of the spectrum of conflict. The PENTOMIC Army was reorganized. No longer focused on the nuclear battlefield, the new Army mission and organization included counterinsurgency and conventional and nuclear war. Such an opportunity for commitment against a low-scale, counterinsurgency threat was emerging in the Republic of Vietnam. In July 1965, the 1st Brigade of the 101st Airborne Division was deployed to Vietnam. Many thought it would be a six-month TDY deployment. In less than eighteen months, the remainder of the division would deploy to Vietnam. The division was gone from Fort Campbell; Fort Campbell was no longer its home. Gone also were the families of the 101st Airborne Division. The old national defense city began a new transition to a basic training city.

CHAPTER 6

THE BASIC TRAINING CITY

1966–1972

There were many changes wrought to our nation, our culture and our Army by the turbulence of the Vietnam years. The decade from 1965 to 1975 is remembered as a time of cultural and sexual revolution, of civic and racial unrest and for the rise of an antiwar protest movement that often turned violent. The stress and strains and the debilitation to the Army and to Army families would take nearly a generation to heal.

The large-scale commitment of U.S. forces to Vietnam brought about change in the city of Fort Campbell. From a national defense city of stable Army families and soldiers living in a predictable routine, the city transformed into a basic training city characterized by the demography of a small professional cadre and a large transient, youthful and single male population that rotated every ten weeks of basic combat training cycles. The transformation was rapid. The 1st Brigade deployed to Vietnam in July 1965. The Basic Combat Training Center opened in May 1966. The remainder of the division deployed to Vietnam in December 1967. All told, the transformation took place in a mere twenty-eight very busy and somewhat confusing months.

The transformation of the city was profound. When the division left, the division *really* left. The severing was complete. There was no rear detachment or sustaining base left at Fort Campbell. Most obviously in terms of transformation, the operational and logistical needs of the division had defined the purpose or mission of the post. The division was the largest unit and population demographic on post. How would the void be filled?

This question was of no small concern to the citizens of the surrounding communities. For one thing, the changing demographics would affect local businesses significantly. A second consequence of the total severing of the division from the city was the total severing of the 101st Airborne Division families from the city. When the soldiers left, their families were no longer authorized family quarters. In a very awkward moment of Army history, the 101st Airborne Division families were essentially evicted from the city. A final and not-too-subtle point about the transformation was that the commander of the 101st Airborne Division was also the commander of Fort Campbell. As the division departed, a new command arrangement needed to be established.

THE BASIC COMBAT TRAINING CENTER: 2 MAY 1966–15 APRIL 1972

As the Vietnam War intensified, so, too, did the need to increase the size of the Army and the size of the training base to train new soldiers. The size of the Army was increased primarily through an expansion of the peacetime draft that had been in place since 1948. The period of service for a draftee was two years, long enough that a drafted soldier could be trained, serve in Vietnam for one year and have five to six months obligation remaining after the Vietnam service. The training base was expanded by identifying existing posts ready, or almost ready, to provide the infrastructure for basic training units. Fort Campbell was nearly ideal for this purpose. There was an existing stock of World War II barracks that could be refurbished. Coincidentally, the 1st Brigade had departed ten months earlier, vacating a significant block of temporary barracks in which it had been housed because of the shortfall of permanent barracks space on the troop line. The ranges and maneuver areas were well maintained and in good shape, though the requirements for basic training would necessitate some additions, modifications and upgrades. There was plenty of room for the 101st Airborne Division, less one brigade, to occupy the old troop line of permanent hammerhead barracks along Kansas Avenue (Desert Storm Boulevard) and for the Basic Combat Training Center to occupy the old World War II barracks between Indiana and Tennessee from 11th to 52nd Streets.

The Basic Combat Training Center was commanded by a brigadier general. He and the training cadre wore the 3rd U.S. Army patch on their left shoulders.

Photo from the *Defender*, the official United States Army Training Center and Fort Campbell newspaper from 1967 to 1972. The *Fort Campbell Courier* continued to publish also. This aerial photograph was taken from the south end of Indiana Boulevard at about 11th Street, looking north along the spine of the old camp layout. The empty field halfway up on the right is the future location of Blanchfield Army Hospital. The crook in the road to the left near the top of the picture would be the intersection of Indiana Avenue and 26th (Screaming Eagle Boulevard).

The headquarters for the Basic Combat Training Center, a two-story World War II building designed to be a regimental headquarters building, was located on Indiana Boulevard just south of 25th Street (Normandy Boulevard) near the center of post. The training center command was made of two training brigades, the 1st Training Brigade and the 2nd Training Brigade. Each training brigade had five training battalions of five companies each. A basic training company had five platoons that accommodated 220 trainees per company per cycle. A captain and two lieutenants were authorized for each training company. The basic training platoons were run by qualified, "Smokey-the-Bear-Campaign-hat-wearing" drill sergeants. The battalions of 1st Training Brigade were located to the south of 26th Street (Screaming Eagle Boulevard), and the battalions of the 2nd Training Brigade were located to the north.

From May 1966 until the commanding general of the 101st Airborne Division, Major General Orlinto

Headquarters, United States Army Training Center, 1967–72.

Barsanti, relinquished command of Fort Campbell, the Basic Combat Training Center was just one of several tenant units under the commanding general 101st Airborne Division and Fort Campbell. Just before the 101st Airborne Division deployed, command of Fort Campbell was turned over to Major General Kelsie L. Reaves, who had just arrived and had been designated to be the first commander of the soon-to-be reactivated 6th Infantry Division. From December 1967 to July 1968, the official stationery heading for the post was "Headquarters 6th Infantry Division and Ft. Campbell." The 6th Division, however, was never formally activated. Plans to do so were dropped in July 1968. A new command arrangement for Fort Campbell became necessary. The new designation for the post became "Headquarters United States Army Training Center and Ft. Campbell (Provisional)." Major General Reaves commanded Fort Campbell and the USATC until September 1968. He was followed by Major General Salve Matteson, Brigadier General John Lekson and then Brigadier General William Birdsong. These four commanders were responsible for running an installation full of tenant organizations, each about their own business. In many ways, their responsibilities harkened back to those of Colonel Guy Chipman and the 1580th Service Command of World War II, the man who described his job to the citizens of Clarksville in 1942 by saying, "I run the big hotel."

The authorized strength of the Basic Combat Training Center was 330 officers, 2,165 enlisted men and 34 civilians. The first commander was Brigadier General Ward Ryan, who had been the assistant division commander of the 101st. The cadre was put together from around the Army, mostly by transfers from U.S. Army, Europe, not from existing strength at Fort Campbell. As the cadre arrived in June, they were newcomers to the city. The cadre had only a short time, sixty days, to prepare to commence training. The cost of refurbishing and preparing the World War II barracks, plus the host of range and training area improvements (physical training areas per battalion, drill fields, an end-of-cycle testing facility, hand-to-hand pits, an infiltration course, a confidence course and obstacle courses), was an astounding $7.5 million expense. A characteristic of this period of the city's history is that a great deal of precious construction and maintenance dollars was diverted to the aging World War II buildings and support of

At the center of the picture is the old Central Issue Facility (CIF) located at Indiana Avenue and 33rd Street. The road to the left is Indiana. The center of the picture is the site of the new PX complex and City Center Park.

the Basic Combat Training Center mission. Little in the way of facilities modernization was funded.

The Army had a very methodical system for the induction of new soldiers. Once selected for the draft and medically screened as fit for service, the draftee reported to a reception station for final inprocessing into the Army and transfer to a basic training station. Ideally, a reception station would be located on the installation where basic training was occurring. For the first several cycles, there was no reception station at Fort Campbell. New soldiers destined to Fort Campbell for basic training were gathered and shipped from other Army reception stations, even as far away as Fort Benning, Georgia. It was a costly and inefficient process, but on 8 August 1966, the United States Army Reception Station (USARECSTA), Fort Campbell, was established. The facility was located on Tennessee Avenue near 27th Street, across the street from the current Don F. Pratt Museum. It was located in World War II temporary buildings and had sufficient housing to accommodate up to one thousand soldiers at a time.

The site of the former U.S. Army Reception Station (1966–72) converted for use as the 101st Airborne Division Replacement Detachment located on Tennessee Avenue across the street from the Pratt Museum.

After the Vietnam years, the old reception station became the welcome center for new arrivals to Fort Campbell. The facility was used until the early 2000s, when the old World War II barracks were torn down and the replacement station was renamed the inprocessing company and relocated to hammerhead barracks on Desert Storm Avenue.

In the six years the training center was active, it graduated over 248,000 basic training–qualified soldiers. The unofficial story of the training center was captured by a weekly eight-page newspaper, the *Defender*, published by the center's public affairs staff for the trainees. It was a quality record of stories and pictures about key personalities, soldiers and the events of daily operations of the training center. The *Defender* took top honors in an Army-wide competition for newspapers of its size and circulation.

As the Vietnam War began to wind down in 1971, the 2nd Training Brigade was deactivated on 10 September 1971. The 1st Training Brigade continued to train new soldiers for another seven months until its operations were ended with a final cycle graduation on 31 March 1972. The Basic Combat Training Center was deactivated on 15 April 1972, a few short weeks before the return of the 101st Airborne Division.

REPLACING THE 101ST AIRBORNE DIVISION: THE 6TH INFANTRY DIVISION, JANUARY–JULY 1968

The commitment of combat troops to Vietnam was incremental but increased steadily from 1965 to 1969. This caused two strategic problems. The first was the need to increase total Army manpower. This was done through the Selective Service System by increasing the draft and then by expanding the number of training bases needed to turn draftees into soldiers through the mechanism of basic training. The second strategic problem was how to backfill the gap in the nation's strategic reserve when active-duty divisions like the 101st Airborne Division were deployed to Vietnam. The 101st Airborne was a key part of the elite Strategic Army Force. Its loss from that command was keenly felt by Army planners.

The secretary of defense, Robert McNamara, announced his solution in September 1967 even as the 101st was deeply involved in final training and preparations for deployment. He announced that the Army would reactivate the 6th Infantry Division at Fort Campbell to replace the 101st as a STRAF division. The plan was halfhearted and very nearly doomed from the start by the complexity of activating a new division on short notice, by a constrained defense budget due to the cost of combat operations in Vietnam and by a personnel assignment strategy that was counterproductive to building a cohesive unit.

The how and when to fill the new division and the how and when to transfer command of the installation were complicated by the enormity of the task, by the sparseness of resources to accomplish the task and by an earlier-than-expected deployment date for the 101st. Due to intelligence warnings about the possibility of a major North Vietnamese army offensive in January 1968, the departure date of the 101st was moved up to December. The 6th Division Headquarters Company, MP Company, Administrative Company and Headquarters Company of the Division Support Command (DISCOM) were hastily activated at Fort Campbell on 24 November 1967. An austere division command post was established under the control of the 6th Infantry Division chief of staff, Colonel John Shoemaker, on 1 December 1967 in Building T-39.[52]

The plan was to activate the 6th Infantry Division, less one brigade. The 3rd Brigade of the division was to be activated in Hawaii to backfill the 25th Division at Schofield Barracks. The division did reach strength of 9,997, or 75 percent, by July. The activation date for the 6th Division was set for 11 May 1968, but on 7 May, the ceremony was postponed indefinitely. Finally, on 3 July, the secretary of defense for the new Nixon administration, Honorable Clark Gifford, cancelled the activation ceremony and removed the 6th Infantry Division from the active division rolls. The new administration had decided to reprioritize and use limited stateside dollars to increase the readiness of the existing Continental Army Command divisions already on active duty. The 6th Infantry Division was closed out with the morning report of 25 July 1968, ending its short eight-month attempt to come to life.[53]

Although the division was not activated, the Army did retain one brigade headquarters, five infantry battalions and one field artillery battalion. This rump organization under the command of a colonel was renamed the Combat Arms Group (Provisional). It became a 3rd U.S. Army tenant unit assigned to Fort Campbell. It did serve a useful purpose in that those many Vietnam "short-timer" returnees could be concentrated in one unit in order to minimize the personnel turbulence they represented in other units. Its primary mission was to train for Vietnam-oriented combat, but the corollary mission was to train as a civil disturbance brigade. Given the social and political turbulence of the time, it was a rather unsavory mission. The Combat Arms Group (Provisional) was deactivated one year later in July 1969.[54]

WAITING WIVES

During the Vietnam War era, a part of preparation for deployment for married soldiers was to find a place for their families to live. Whether a soldier was deploying with his unit or, as was more likely the case after 1968, as an individual replacement, his family was not authorized family quarters at the current installation of assignment. Where to move the family was stressful enough, but in a time of stress and anxiety, in the coming year of worry about the safety of the soldier in a war zone, the family was separated from all the usual support provided by an Army community: wives clubs, church groups, school mates, Scouts and even just the plain old comforting common society of those who understood and knew Army life.

In late 1965 through 1966, an unusual effort took place to address this problem. Schilling Air Force Base, Kansas, was closing. The entire base was being boarded up. There were 790 sets of unoccupied but very usable quarters. The base commander, Colonel John (Mike) Scanlon, noticing that the 1st Infantry Division at nearby Fort Riley was deploying, developed a plan to allow Army families of deploying soldiers to move into the quarters. Scanlon actively sought approval for his plan through the Air Force chain of command. Approval was quick in coming and further caught the attention of Kansas senator Bob Dole. Schilling Manor, as it thereafter was named, became an extremely unusual place, a home to families of deployed soldiers, sailors and airmen. The story of the Schilling Manor experience and that of the fate of many Army families was fairly well overlooked during the Vietnam War. It has only recently been told, and told very well, by Donna Moreau in her 2005 memoir, *Waiting Wives: The Story of Schilling Manor, Home Front to the Vietnam War.*[55]

It took time, but the Schilling Manor solution took hold across the Department of Defense. On many installations, the deployments of units had left many sets of empty quarters. Fort Campbell was one of those installations. As the program evolved, when a service member received orders to Vietnam, the family could apply for waiting wives quarters at any available installation. Locations were chosen by families for a wide variety of reasons: proximity to family, familiarity with the installation, next assignment, etc. At most installations, waiting wives were integrated in and among the residents of an appropriate housing area based on rank. They were not segregated into a specific "waiting wives" area. The waiting wives were not a homogeneous group. Perhaps the only thing they had in common with other waiting wives families was that their sponsors were assigned to Vietnam. At Fort Campbell, a waiting wives coffee group was formed and monthly social activities were planned.

PLANNING FOR THE HOMECOMING

At Fort Campbell and in the surrounding communities, it had been assumed that the 101st would certainly redeploy back to Fort Campbell. The post engineer and his staff had already begun the process of evaluating the transition back from a basic training city. There had been some significant changes in the organization of the 101st while it was in Vietnam. The division was bringing home a new name: the 101st Airborne Division (Airmobile). With that new parenthetical identifier of "Airmobile" came four hundred more helicopters in need of ramp space and hangars, several hundred more warrant officer pilots who were authorized company grade quarters and several hundred more soldiers in need of permanent troop housing. When the Department of Defense gave the word of the homecoming in early 1972, the post engineer dropped his prepared request for $26.3 million of upgrades.

The staff of the House Appropriations Committee caught sight of the large request and put the brakes on it. The staff recommended to the committee that an alternate, Fort Stewart, Georgia, with nearby Hunter Army Airfield, would be a better-suited and less-costly alternative. An intensive lobby effort from Tennessee and Kentucky congressional delegations and local political leaders from Clarksville and Hopkinsville supported the Army staff who argued in favor of Fort Campbell. Although Fort Stewart was 100,000 acres larger than Fort Campbell and Hunter Army Airfield already had facilities to house four hundred helicopters, Fort Stewart lacked adequate housing for the division, now numbering seventeen thousand soldiers. By objective analysis, it was proven to the committee that to upgrade housing at Fort Stewart would actually cost $50 million more than to execute the required upgrades at Fort Campbell. The Army prevailed, Congress relented and an official homecoming ceremony was held at Campbell Army Airfield on 6 April 1972. Fourteen thousand dignitaries and well-wishers were on hand. A division change of command between Major General Thomas Tarpley, the outgoing commander, and Major General John Cushman took place. Upon assuming command of the division, General Cushman also assumed command of Fort Campbell. The 101st Airborne Division (Airmobile) and the city of Fort Campbell had now come full circle. A new transformation was about to begin.[56]

CHAPTER 7

AN ARMY OF EXCELLENCE CITY

1972–2004

The Army of 1972, the Army that returned from Vietnam, was an Army "cloaked in anguish." It was an institution fighting to maintain its existence in the midst of a growing national apathy, decay and intolerance. As a microcosm of the larger society, racial discord poured out of the barracks and even into the streets of Army housing areas and local military communities. Drug use was rampant, especially in Europe, where 40 percent of soldiers admitted to the use of marijuana and hashish. Military discipline and respect for NCO and officer authority was at an all-time low; 12 percent of soldiers in Europe in 1972 were charged with serious breaches of the Uniform Code of Military Justice. A 1973 Harris Poll revealed that the American public ranked the military only above sanitation workers in relative order of merit. In the midst of this turmoil, Congress brought to an end the Selective Service draft and the Army began the experiment with an all-volunteer Army, a project with the acronym VOLAR.[57]

The nation recovered from the "crisis of confidence" brought about by the "distraction of the Vietnam decade," and so, too, did the armed forces. In the case of the Army, its road to recovery was guided by a remarkable group of senior leaders who developed an intellectual framework for reform called the Army of Excellence (AOE). Briefly, the AOE required the Army to change its fundamental character from that of a mass conscription citizens army of the World War II, Korea and Vietnam eras to a smaller Army made of volunteer, high-quality and long-serving professionals. High-technology weapons and command systems, professional education and sound doctrinal development were certainly part of the AOE transformation, but at the core of the ability to use high-tech equipment and to execute complex doctrine with great agility was the personnel component of quality soldiers and exceptional leaders.[58]

The distraction of the Vietnam decade had a very visible effect on the city of Fort Campbell. Dollars diverted to maintain hundreds of World War II barracks and building ranges and facilities unique to basic training were dollars diverted from developing the city and upgrading infrastructure. It was as if the city had to stand still for a decade. In a sense, the basic training city retarded the growth of the future city that beginning in 1972 would have to undergo a transformation to support the Army of Excellence. It was not long before the complimentary term "An Army Community of Excellence" began to be heard. Efforts to reform the city paralleled efforts to reform the Army. A quality, professional Army of Excellence deserved nothing less.

REFORM WELL BEGUN: VOLAR AND THE AIR ASSAULT SPIRIT, 1972–1980

There were challenges to rebuilding the division. Recruiting enough new all-volunteer soldiers to bring the severely under-strength division up to strength, training them and validating their training as a combat-ready division was a huge challenge that was accomplished within a year. To celebrate the accomplishment, General Cushman instituted a celebration called Week of the Eagles. The weeklong celebration of sports challenges, air shows, soldier and equipment demonstrations, a formal dining-out and a division review has become an annual tradition since, though sometimes it is forgotten just what it is that this celebration honors.

A priority was to transform the city as home for the 101st Airborne Division (Airmobile). Among many competing construction requirements, the development of aviation operation and maintenance facilities was critical. The outline and preparation of these projects had preceded the return of the division. The shortage of facilities was so acute that the division's air cavalry squadron, 2-17 Cavalry, had to park and operate its helicopters from an open field in the middle of the recently vacated Clarksville Base. In its new role, the base took on the nickname "Cav Country." For housing, the squadron occupied the former Marine Corps barracks in the center of the old base, a very comfortable facility isolated from main post and the prying eyes of "higher headquarters." The cavalry troopers led a fine life "far from the flagpole," as the soldiers say. A significant expansion of Campbell Army Airfield (CAAF) ramps, hangars, tarmac, control towers and other facilities was undertaken. Even with the CAAF expansion, a second airfield was required. It was built four miles south of the cantonment along Woodlawn Road. It was named Saber Army Airfield because it became the new home of the cavalry squadron's helicopter fleet.

Providing appropriate troop housing for unmarried enlisted soldiers of the emerging all-volunteer Army was a top priority also. Open-bay housing was appropriate for a conscripted Army but not for an all-volunteer Army. A first solution was the modification of existing hammerhead and temporary barracks housing to provide for four-man rooms for enlisted and private rooms with baths for NCOs living in the barracks. Soldiers were given greater autonomy to exercise their own taste in decorating and arranging their more private quarters. Young soldiers tended toward the fashionable trends of the day. Volcano lamps, black lights, pop icon posters

A soldier's room from the VOLAR era.

and beads predominated. The news media delighted in highlighting the new all-volunteer Army as a kind of adjunct to the youth culture. Media attention gave the impression that the VOLAR program was nothing more than a misplaced acquiescence to such. It was a mistaken impression, and in time, the novelty wore off.[59]

Major General Cushman initiated a program named Operation Improve in order to better the infrastructure and operations of the city. The operation in and of itself was not novel; what was new, however, was that General Cushman solicited criticism and input in the forum of open town hall meetings. Representatives of the division and garrison staffs were on hand to hear and discuss issues. The first Fort Campbell town hall meeting was held on 22 March 1972. Such meetings have become a routine part of Army community living ever since. One of the most serious complaints aired early in the process was the availability of family housing. No new family housing had been built since Stryker Village in 1962. Congress had forsaken the Wherry and Capehart privatization programs in 1962. New housing construction in the absence of privatization programs would be expensive and require appropriated MILCON (military construction) dollars. It took a fight and a number of budget cycles in Washington, D.C., but with support from Tennessee and Kentucky congressional delegations, funding was provided by 1978 for expansion of a number of NCO quarters in Hammond Heights and two new enlisted and NCO housing areas, Pierce Village and La Pointe Village.[60] A number of on-post services and facilities were planned and funded. Branch exchanges located in the troop housing areas, two new brigade gymnasiums, an indoor pool (Gardner Pool on Indiana Avenue) and a new, modern commissary located in the center of the city near the main PX highlighted the early commitment to upgrade facilities.

National security policy determines the mission and organization of the Army. The new Nixon Doctrine (1969) began to move the Army away from a focus on the counterinsurgency, small-unit, guerrilla warfare operations in Vietnam for which the 101st Airborne Division (Airmobile) was so renowned. The new post-Vietnam national security focus was on forward defense of Europe and the mid- to high-intensity operations envisioned against modern Soviet-equipped and trained forces. The problem was how to convert the 101st into a capable anti-tank force relevant to the European environment. The answer was the development of a new kind of division that could capitalize on emerging doctrine and especially on new technologies. Well before the AOE doctrine and new equipment was available, the division had already begun a period of dynamic experimentation that resulted in the air assault doctrine.

Major General Sidney Berry embraced the air assault concept and sought to rally the division around a new character and a new attitude called "Air Assault!" A concept for retraining the division in these new air assault skills was conceived in January 1974. A group of officers in the division outlined a plan for converting the existing Airborne School on post to an Air Assault School. Shortly thereafter, a Program of Instruction (POI) for an Air Assault School was approved by General Berry. Air transportability skills, rappelling and tough physical conditioning standards were part of a challenging program that earned the nickname "the ten toughest days in the Army." Under supervision of the Division G3, an Air Assault School cadre was selected and trained. An obstacle course, twelve- and thirty-four-foot rappelling towers and other necessary modifications for the new course of instruction were made to the old Airborne School. The first Air Assault School graduation and the presentation of the first air assault badges took place on 7 April 1974. In order to further enhance the air assault spirit, General Berry adopted the wearing of a dark blue air assault beret in place of the garrison hat and the fatigue baseball hat. In December 1974, the division changed the parenthetical title from "(Airmobile)" to "(Air Assault)." On 6 January 1978, the Army formally accredited the Air Assault School and authorized wear of the air assault badge Army wide. The air assault blue beret, like a number of other unofficial berets that popped up throughout the Army in the late 1970s, was squashed by the army chief of staff in 1979 and passed unceremoniously into history.[61] The adoption of the air assault concept was significant in the life and character of the city. The spirit of the division became a part of the spirit of a newly revitalized installation. Fort Campbell became the home of the "world's only air assault division."

The construction of the decade of the 1970s finished with two significant quality-of-life projects. The old Station Hospital, a workhorse since 1942, had outlived its useful life as a medical facility. A new, modern hospital was planned and funded to take its place. The new hospital was more than just a welcome necessity. It was symbolic of the nation's growing commitment to providing quality healthcare for the soldiers and family members of the all-volunteer force. It was intended to be indicative of a commitment to provide a better environment in which long-serving Army families could flourish. It was formally dedicated on 17 September 1982 in honor of the first female chief of the Army Nurse Corps, Colonel Florence A. Blanchfield.

Blanchfield Army Hospital, 1988.

The second significant project that finished out the decade of 1970s construction was that of two new brigade-sized troop housing areas. Oddly enough, no one seems to remember an architectural design name for these compounds. Soldiers called them the "college dorms" or the "VOLAR barracks." The areas were built on the north end of the cantonment between Tennessee and Indiana. The first was completed in 1977–78 between 50th and 53rd Streets; the second was completed in 1982 and was located between 56th and 59th Streets. They are currently the home of the 1st Brigade Combat Team and the 2nd Brigade Combat Team, respectively. The design of the compounds was contemporary for the late 1970s. The barracks and associated buildings were built symmetrically around a large, open parklike area. The barracks were three-story structures with four three-man rooms per floor. The rooms shared a common area, but each had a private bath. Separate buildings around the perimeter were built as company supply/ arms rooms; each battalion had a building that housed the company orderly rooms in a line HHC to D, a battalion headquarters building that housed two battalion headquarters (the third battalion of each brigade had to utilize other buildings for a makeshift headquarters). Each brigade area had a large dining facility (notice that it was not called a mess hall) seating 350 at a time. Each brigade had a brigade headquarters building. A joint service club and modernistic designed chapel (Memorial Chapel) were shared by the two brigades. The 1st and 2nd Brigades occupied the VOLAR areas. The 3rd Brigade, the Division Support Command (DISCOM), Division Artillery (DIVARTY) and the separate battalions occupied the hammerheads of the old troop line.[62]

THE ARMY OF EXCELLENCE COMES TO FRUITION: 1980–1992

The Army senior leadership began to roll out the Army of Excellence reforms in early 1980. A part of the context for a decade of reform was the revitalization of the American spirit and an economy that began to boom by 1984. The Army attracted quality high school–graduate, professionally oriented recruits. Pay and incentives began a climb toward parity with civilian professions. The administration and Congress were committed to providing substantial funding to support the reform. The validation of the investment in the Army of Excellence was the spectacular victory in the 1990–91 Gulf War. There is an old saying that the surest catalyst to reform is disaster. The Army of the immediate post-Vietnam years was a disaster. When giving testimony to the Senate Armed Services Committee after the 1990–91 Gulf War, Major General Barry McCaffery was asked how it was that the war was won in only one hundred hours. He replied, "This war didn't take 100 hours to win, it took 15 years."[63]

The AOE reforms were holistic. It was not just a matter of better recruits and pay. Education, technology, doctrine and training were crafted and interwoven in the quest to develop a small, professional and agile Army designed to win the first battle of the next war decisively. Battle Dress Uniforms (BDUs) and the High-Mobility Multipurpose Wheeled Vehicle (HMMWV) were distinctive, visible changes from the old OD Green/Willy's Jeep Army of the past seventy years. The newest and most capable Army helicopters—the UH-60 Black Hawk, AH-64 Apaches and CH-47D helicopters—filled the skies above and around Fort Campbell, making the conceptualization of air assault doctrine a reality. Deployments to the National Training Centers (JRTC and NTC) provided exceptionally realistic training against a world-class and interactive opposing force; many said a trip to one of the readiness centers was tougher than real combat. An emphasis on equally demanding home-station training complemented biannual battalion deployments to the training centers. Fighting the first battle and winning decisively was the goal of AOE, but a side product was an Army growing intensely proud and professional.

A part of the new sights on the installation in the 1980s were the Green Berets of the 5th Special Forces Group (Airborne) and the maroon berets of Task Force 160, latter renamed the 160th Special Operations Aviation Regiment (Airborne). Both units were a reflection of the AOE initiatives. Task Force 160 was formed as a result of the disaster of Desert One in the Iranian hostage rescue attempt of April 1980. Because of that disaster, the Department of Defense tasked the Army with putting together an elite helicopter unit to support special operating forces. The Army came to Fort Campbell in 1981 to recruit and train the task force because of the number and types of helicopters in the air assault division and the highly trained pilots, crew chiefs and mechanics who operated them. The 5th Group had been stationed at Fort Bragg, North Carolina, but because of the increasing importance and number of Special Forces Groups, Fort Bragg was just not big enough for all the groups. The 5th Group was selected for transfer and arrived at Fort Campbell in June 1988. The geographic and cultural area of expertise of 5th Group was the Middle East and Central Asia.

The special operations units added to the character of the AOE city. Since the stationing of the 11th Airborne Division at Camp Campbell in 1948, the city had a distinctive airborne culture. The transition of the division to the "World's Only Air Assault Division," the operation of the Army's Air Assault School, the presence of the 86th Combat Support Hospital (Airborne) and the addition of special operating forces that also made use of the third dimension of the battlefield—the skies—further accentuated a distinct characteristic of the city of Fort Campbell, the home of the Army's most elite vertical envelopment forces.

THE HOMEFRONT OF OPERATION DESERT SHIELD/ DESERT STORM

Saddam Hussein invaded Kuwait on 2 August 1990. In less than forty-eight hours, his Republican Guard divisions had overrun Kuwait and were poised to take oil-rich Saudi Arabia. President George H.W. Bush declared, "This will not stand, this aggression against Kuwait." The division was alerted on 7 August, its first battalion deployed on 17 August and the remainder of the division closed in Saudi Arabia by 25 September. The record of events in Operation Desert Shield/Desert Storm speaks for itself. It was a magnificent operation, a real vindication of the AOE initiatives of more than a decade.

The city of Fort Campbell had its role to play in the victory too. Long gone was the notion that an Army post was merely a place for a unit to live until it deployed, as was the case in the Vietnam era. The role of the installation in the AOE era was to assist in deployment and sustainment of the division, operate a rear detachment Emergency Operations Center (EOC) to coordinate with the division rear detachment, take command of the installation and sustain community operations and operate the garrison as a mobilization station for National Guard and Army Reserve units readying for deployment. Years of practice had gone into rehearsing these functions. Procedures had been codified, especially in the division's Readiness Standard Operating Procedures (RSOP). This deployment to Saudi Arabia in August 1990 was the "big one." This was the event that everyone had been training for. It stressed and tested every fiber of the installation's readiness capabilities.

Since the first days of the reactivation of the 101st Airborne Division (PENTOMIC) in 1956, that division that was Skilled, Tough, Ready to go Around the Clock (STRAC), emergency deployment has been part of the culture of the city. Beginning with its return from Vietnam as the 101st Airborne Division (Airmobile), every major combat exercise on post began with a simulated emergency alert and deployment sequence. Unannounced readiness inspections called EDREs (Emergency Readiness Deployment Exercises) kept everyone on their toes. Rapid deployment and the Rapid Deployment Force (RDF) was part of the XVIII Airborne Corps culture of which the 101st was part. The deployment to Saudi Arabia, however, was not a test and not just a battalion or brigade effort; it was the whole division and all the other deployable units on the installation. In the six weeks between 17 August and 25 September 1990, Fort Campbell deployed over eighteen thousand soldiers—with all their equipment, supplies and initial issue of ammunition—and 5,258 pieces of equipment halfway around the world.[64]

It was an amazing feat. It was all the more amazing because it was done with an infrastructure that was essentially unimproved since the 1950s. Hundreds of vehicles and rolling stock were loaded on flat cars from concrete ramps along Wickham Avenue that could accommodate no more than five train cars at a time. The majority of the rail loading took place track side in a barren field called Caskey Crossing four miles north of the installation.

Diesel generators provided power for lights at night. Soldiers were fed from Vietnam-era marmite cans under canvas tents. Linking the loaded train cars together from the Army's rail line between Fort Campbell and Hopkinsville to the main CSX rail line for the trip to Jacksonville, Florida, was accomplished through a rail interchange yard in Hopkinsville that could accommodate only ten cars at a time. The painfully cumbersome process blocked traffic in downtown Hopkinsville every time a ten-car segment was transferred to the main line. Once the trains arrived at the port, the equipment was transferred to ten reserve fleet Navy cargo ships that were so old that one of them, the *American Eagle*, had transported the division's equipment to Vietnam in 1967. Unit equipment not traveling by train to Jacksonville was loaded into 1,500- by 120-foot intermodal sea-land containers. The containers were staged at various improvised locations near the unit areas and loaded onto a fleet of contracted flatbed tractor-trailer trucks for the trip to the port. The only relatively new part of the deployment process was the self-deployment of helicopters. The division's fleet of helicopters flew to Jacksonville. In Florida, the aircraft were partially disassembled and prepared for deployment in a shrink-wrap plastic for the journey aboard ship with the rolling stock, containers and vehicles.[65]

The equipment moving by sea preceded the soldiers who were deployed by air. The timing was such that the soldiers would arrive in Saudi Arabia at about the same time as their seaborne equipment. Deployment from the airfield was essentially unchanged since the 1950s. Soldiers staged in their unit areas until called forward. They moved to the airfield by fleets of Army buses and waited outside on the tarmac until called to load. If there was a delay, the soldiers waited on the tarmac. There were no facilities at the airfield to accommodate waiting soldiers except for an empty hangar or two.

Rather than as was the case with the Vietnam deployment, the division remained tethered to Fort Campbell. Command of the garrison was transferred from the division commander, Major General Binford Peay, to the garrison commander when Peay deployed. The division and the garrison ran a joint Emergency Operations Center in the basement of Building 95, the Coiner Signal Building. The joint center was staffed by representatives from all installation agencies and division staff sections. The ad hoc arrangement worked very well, but it did require the division to make decisions about who to leave behind to run rear detachment operations. Both ends of the operation were critical, yet the Table of Organization and Equipment (TO&E) did not consider split operations like this.

As part of the AOE reforms, the Army had moved toward a better functional organization and integration of National Guard and Army Reserve units. The effort was called the "Total Army." The capabilities and functions that the Army needed while deployed to an austere theater, but not for day-to-day operations, were placed in the Army Reserve. Engineer construction units, water and fuel pipeline units and bath and laundry units were the types found in the Reserve. Their skills and equipment were essential for victory in the desert. Pre-planning deployment scenarios and annual training were rather mundane tasks handled by the Installation Deputy for Plans, Training and Mobilization (DPTMS) over the years, but the planning and the relationships developed between Guard/Reserve units and the installation staff were critical to a smooth mobilization operation when it happened in 1990–91. The mobilization procedure through Fort Campbell was a three-week process that included initial organization, equipment issue and inspection, pre-deployment training requirements and preparation of personnel and equipment for deployment. Thousands of Guard and Reserve soldiers were mobilized and deployed through Fort Campbell.

When the division and other units deployed, Fort Campbell became overnight one of the largest single-parent communities in the United States. The challenge was profound. School staffs, installation chaplains, Army community services, moral recreation and welfare, the Red Cross, Army emergency relief, the law enforcement command, Blanchfield Army Hospital and the garrison commander, with the help of the spouses of the senior commanders and NCOs, had quite a job on their hands. In spite of the many services that were available, the Army had traditionally depended, informally, on Army wives—usually the wives of the company commander and the first sergeant—to organize and take care of the basic needs of young wives and their families struggling through the stress of a deployment. In an odd anomaly, but one that was significant enough to make a noticeable negative impact, many mid-grade officer and NCO families simply picked up and went home for the duration. The wives and families of junior enlisted soldiers could not afford that luxury. The departure of so many families from the Fort Campbell area also had a significant negative impact on the local economy.[66]

A FORCE PROJECTION PLATFORM: 1992–2003

In the background of the immediate concern of Operation Desert Shield/ Desert Storm was the ongoing and now nearly complete collapse of the old Soviet Union. The Soviet military threat in Europe had been the focus of U.S. foreign policy and the threat that the AOE initiatives had worked to counter. The new international situation caused a profound reassessment of the situation and moved the Army focus from reinforcing a forward deployed force in Europe to one that would be an expeditionary, power projection Army deployed from stateside installations against a variety of yet-to-be-defined threats. Army doctrine writers struggled with a host of potential missions that were loosely grouped as Military Operations Other Than War, or MOOTW, pronounced *moot-wah*.[67]

As ambiguous as MOOTWA missions might have been in the early 1990s, the way ahead for the installation was clear. Three core competencies were developed: power projection, mission training and well-being. As a result of the Desert Shield/Desert Storm deployment experience, upgrading deployment infrastructure was a necessity. The critical rail deployment upgrade was the first priority. A rail operations facility was built at the southeast corner of the cantonment. The facility provided an all-weather hardstand staging area for 900 vehicles, a command and control building and a lighted railhead with ten ramps for handling 20 cars each. The ramp configuration made it possible to load 240 railcars per day. In conjunction with the rail operations facility located at Fort Campbell, a new railroad connector interchange was built south of Hopkinsville at the other end of the Army railroad line. With absolutely no disruption to Hopkinsville traffic, the rail connector interchange facility could handle the transfer of 100 loaded railcars in thirty minutes. Line haul, the use of contracted tractor-trailer trucks to transport intermodal containers to Jacksonville, was enhanced by providing all-weather staging areas for each brigade and the purchase of additional material-handling equipment (MHE) to increase truck-loading operations to a pace of 160 trucks per day. Millions of dollars were poured into airfield improvements. The building of a passenger processing facility, essentially a modern airline terminal, for the staging and receiving of deployed troops greatly enhanced the installation's ability to provide quality service for a power projection Army.

While the headquarters building, the reliable T-39, and the Coiner Signal Building, Building 95 built in 1952, made do as rear detachment command and control facilities in 1990, both were well past time for an

The rail facility.

upgrade, which was made necessary not only by the new mission but also because of tremendous leaps in worldwide command and control technologies. T-39 was retained as a historic building and continues to serve, appropriately so, as the garrison headquarters. For command and control of garrison emergency operations, however, a new Emergency Operations Center (EOC) has been built. The division headquarters moved out of T-39 in 2006 and occupied a new, thoroughly modern facility located three blocks north of T-39 on Indiana Avenue. Across the street from the new headquarters location, within a triangle formed by the new headquarters, the new consolidated soldier in- and out-processing center (the newly refurbished 1978 commissary building) and the new PX is a small park that has been named City Center Park. In some sense, the center of the city shifted with the move of the division headquarters to a new location, but in a historic sense, the center of the city still remains at T-39. Operation Desert Shield/Desert Storm highlighted the importance of the U.S. Army Reserves. Because of the importance of the Army Reserve to worldwide contingency operations, a new Armed Forces Reserve Center was built on the installation. It is a building very much like a command and control center and provides a central location for managing all aspects of Reserve unit training and mobilization at Fort Campbell.

The new (2006) 101st Airborne Division (Air Assault) Division Headquarters overlooking Indiana Avenue.

A much more difficult problem to fix was that of the strange anomaly of mid-grade career families fleeing Fort Campbell during the Desert Shield/ Desert Storm deployment. Clearly the phenomenon was not healthy for an expeditionary Army expecting a greater number of small-unit deployments in the coming years. It was not a problem that could be fixed by an infrastructure upgrade.

The phenomenon was not unique to Fort Campbell; it was an Army-wide problem. Army senior leadership gave it much attention. The result was the formation of Family Readiness Groups (FRGs). Unit commanders at the battalion and company level and their spouses were encouraged to foster an organization of family members, volunteers, soldiers and civilian employees associated with their unit. The goals of the FRGs included providing families with practical tools for adjusting to military deployments and separations, fostering family resiliency and acting as an extension of the unit in providing accurate command information to the families of deployed soldiers.

The professional Army produced by the AOE initiatives, the upgrades made to the deployment infrastructure in order to support an expeditionary Army and the building of resilient Army families in a supportive military community came to a test on 11 September 2001. Shortly after that brutal attack on the nation's homeland, 5th Special Forces Group, the 160th and the 3rd Brigade Combat Team of the 101st Airborne Division (Air Assault) deployed to locations in and around Afghanistan. For the first time, all three Fort Campbell units operated together. The power of the Taliban was quickly broken, but a new threat emerged in Iraq. In February 2002, the division was alerted for deployment to Iraq for what became known as Operation Iraqi Freedom.

The division deployed from Fort Campbell in only ten days. The deployment process was exceptional. Twenty-three thousand soldiers with all their equipment and rolling stock deployed to Saudi Arabia, halfway around the world, in little over one week. The weather that February at Fort Campbell was awful. It was, however, a minimal inconvenience. Rail, line haul, helicopter self-deployment and the marshalling of soldiers at the airfield were smooth and unhampered. Hardstand surfaces and other conveniences that had been built into the facilities made the difference. As if to highlight the joint nature of the improvements throughout the armed forces that had taken place since Desert Shield/Desert Storm, the division's equipment was speedily loaded onto four of the Navy's newest roll-on/roll-off ships. The division received its equipment in theater, configured it for combat and crossed the line of departure into Iraq on 21 March 2003, only weeks after the deployment began.[68]

This time the division's families did not flee Fort Campbell. The FRG effort and community initiatives provided a supportive environment. Families stayed, and it was their extended families that came to Fort Campbell to support their loved ones by being here with them. So significant was the presence of extended family members in the Fort Campbell area that local merchants reported an increase in sales, business and profits during the deployment. It was a rather dramatic reversal of the situation that had occurred twelve years earlier and a testimony to the FRG effort, the Fort Campbell installation staff and the leaders of the local communities around Fort Campbell. The division returned from Iraq beginning in March 2004.

CHAPTER 8

A WORLD-CLASS ARMY HOME

2004–2014

One autumn day in 2008, the garrison commander, Colonel Fred Swope, came to work after an evening of reflecting on the considerable progress that was being made to facilities and services across the city of Fort Campbell. Colonel Swope met with the garrison staff and shared with them his deep impression that Fort Campbell was fast becoming what he called a "world-class Army home." The phrase stuck with the staff and soon became the official motto. It expressed Colonel Swopes's vision that the Fort Campbell experience should become the standard of quality in the professional memory of all who served there. The motto has since been enshrined on historic Gate 3. Colonel Swope's impression in 2008 could only be made after years and years of hard work by those who served before him. Facilities and infrastructure were in need of upgrading at the close of the 1990s. It took a lot of hard work to get to the point of being able to appreciate the visible progress taking shape in the city by the year 2008.

When the division came home from Iraq in March 2004, it was faced with two major projects. The first was to recover men, gear and equipment from a year of grueling combat in one of the world's harshest environments and to "reset," or make ready to do it again. The second task was to undergo a reorganization called Army transformation. Army transformation was a modernization plan aiming to move the Army away from its Cold War, AOE, divisional orientation to a newer organization structure made of modular brigade combat teams. The new structure was designed to provide for flexible, fully functional brigade combat teams of about three thousand soldiers. The concept was to enable the Army to conduct the continuous operations that the Global War on Terror was going to demand. The effect was that the return home in 2004 was the last time in over a decade that the 101st Airborne Division (Air Assault) would move and act together as a single division. From 2005 to 2014, division headquarters deployed four times to provide command and control for a number of modular brigades that were not of the 101st, just as the brigade combat teams have also deployed multiple time each as modular brigades under the command and control of division headquarters other than the 101st.

As a result of these many and varied modular unit deployments, the city was in a state of flux. Half the division might be deployed at any one time while the other half was in a state of recovery and reset pending the next deployment already on the horizon. Brigades would return, and then other brigades would deploy. It was a stressful time for soldiers and families in which a routine of a one-year deployment was followed by a one-year recovery that was followed by the deployment cycle over again.

In the midst of ongoing organizational transformation and multiple deployments, the city entered a period of transformation also. The city has long been a home for soldiers and Army families. A core competency for the installation was well-being of the soldier and his family, of which safe, adequate housing had been a central concern. It had been, however, many, many years since the physical homes, the dwellings, for both unaccompanied soldiers and family housing had been upgraded. The last major improvement to unaccompanied soldier housing had been the VOLAR upgrades of the 1970s. The last major improvement to family housing had been the addition of the Pierce and La Pointe Housing areas in the late 1970s.

The problem was Army-wide, and it was known to be a key factor in soldier satisfaction. It was known that there was a direct correlation between satisfaction with housing and reenlistment and retention. One could almost hear the echoes of the voice of Secretary of Defense Louis Johnson from the early 1950s: "There is nothing more vital or pressing in the interest of morale and security of America than proper housing for our Armed Forces." It was "déjà vu all over again."

THE ARMY BARRACKS MASTER PLAN

Soldier barracks are constructed and maintained with Army dollars. The cost associated with barracks construction and maintenance competed with budget requirements for operations, readiness and training. It became apparent by 1994 that priority was going to have to be given to correcting the problem of aging, dysfunctional and inadequate soldier housing.

The barracks modernization program got off to a slow start, but the first effects of it were felt at Fort Campbell as early as 1994. The first sets of modern barracks were built north of the old cantonment area and south of the airfield. It was terrain in the near vicinity of what had been Son Drop Zone. The barracks modernization project took a specific approach to develop a brigade complex of barracks and the associated facilities of company operations areas, motor pools, dining facilities and buildings for battalion and a brigade headquarters. The idea of a complex was that all the facilities necessary for the operation of a brigade would be within walking distance of the soldiers living in the complex. The Army's barracks complex idea served as a starting point for the Fort Campbell Real Property Planning Board to expand the given complex into what was called a "brigade footprint." A brigade footprint would ensure that installation planners included the shopping and health conveniences, physical fitness facilities and other recreation and entertainment venues also within walking distance of the complex. Each brigade complex would attain a certain level of autonomy and self-sufficiency.

A second brigade complex was begun in 1996 for the 3rd Brigade that had been housed in the renovated hammerhead barracks along Desert Storm Avenue between 21st and 25th Streets. The cantonment area was flat out of any open space for construction, so for the first time since the early 1960s, a part of previous construction needed to be torn down to make way for the new. The new brigade complex was built right on the same terrain after the removal of the hammerheads. In FY 1999, a third barracks complex was funded for the Division Support Command (DISCOM). The DISCOM area was located south of the 3rd Brigade area on the old troop line. Construction in the area necessitated the moving of the Air Assault School from its grounds on the original Airborne School to its current and more spacious location four blocks to the west on what is now called Air Assault Boulevard (the former 18th Street). It was during this time of construction that the division commander, Major General Robert Clark, asked the Installation Memorialization Committee to consider renaming many of the main roads around the cantonment to names reminiscent of the battles and campaigns of the 101st Airborne Division. The plan broke the flow of the old street grid of 1942 but did add a colorful and historical twist.

The barracks modernization plan established a standard for soldier comfort and privacy. The standard was called 1+1. The standard was to provide for junior enlisted soldiers a module that provided for two private bedrooms with closets and a shared bathroom and service area. Junior NCOs in the grade of E5 and E6 would be authorized the entire module. The Army was successful in demonstrating the program to Congress, and in FY 2001, Congress added $550 million to the defense budget for Quality of Life Enhancement. The program was extended through 2014. Funds continued to be provided for the modernization program.[69]

The installation pushed forward with an aggressive barracks-building program. Space management for the brigade footprints was a challenge because every square foot on the old cantonment was allotted. Space was at a premium. New brigade complexes for 5th Special Forces Group (2005) and 16th SOAR (2006) were built on the north side of the original spine of the cantonment area along Wickham (Missouri) and Tennessee Avenues between 33rd and 42nd Streets. What buildings and facilities had been there were removed to make room for the new. The need for space and the continued building simply burst the boundaries of the old cantonment. A brigade complex for the 157th Combat Aviation Brigade was built well outside the old cantonment on ground never used before south of old Clarksville Base just off Woodlawn Drive (2007), and the brigade complex built for the 52nd Explosive Ordnance Brigade was within the boundary of the old Clarksville Base (2010). Construction of unaccompanied soldier housing will continue until the goal of the program, to provide 1+1 housing for all unaccompanied soldiers, is met.

THE RESIDENTIAL COMMUNITIES INITIATIVE

By the late 1990s, the condition of Army family housing at Fort Campbell was dismal, the same word that was used in 1950 to describe the assortment of temporary housing available then. The building and maintenance of family housing was always a difficult issue to solve. Since the end of the Wherry-Capehart era in 1962, the Army had tried to meet the need with MILCON money. It was a failing methodology. But as adequate and

Modern Army family housing intended to compete in comfort and appearance with housing in the civilian sector.

appropriate housing was correlated to soldier satisfaction and reenlistment rates, doubly so was the correlation with adequate and appropriate family housing with a professional career path for married soldiers. Through the 1990s, Fort Campbell applied well-intentioned but Band-Aid-like repairs and upgrades to the stock of Wherry- and Capehart-era housing. That housing was considered "affordable" in the 1950s. By 2000, the Capehart Ranch-style home was derisively nicknamed a "brick single wide," a status even lower than "affordable."

The answer to solving the Army family housing crisis was to be found in privatization, like that used in the 1950s. Several attempts were made in the 1980s by the Reagan administration to reinvigorate a privatization scheme, but they did not come to fruition. Fortunately, successive administrations were favorable to finding a solution. The Clinton administration program to "reinvent government" and the Bush program to outsource as many government functions better suited to the private sector kept the impetus for finding a private-sector solution alive.

Privatization was a controversial idea. Those with severe reservations about turning the whole housing program over to private developers included congressmen, senior Army leaders and many garrison commanders. Several pilot programs were initiated on selected Army installations, and the results when measured by soldier and family satisfaction were more than just favorable. The program was a success. One of the Army leaders who was instrumental in promoting the program was the vice chief of staff, General Jack Keene. General Keene brought much insight and passion as an advocate for the program from his many years of service at Fort Campbell, including those as commander of the 101st Airborne Division (Air Assault) and at Fort Campbell in the early 1990s, when family housing was in a grim state in need of a solution.

In 2003, Fort Campbell elected to participate in the program. The contract for privatization was awarded to a very successful participant in the program with a proven track record, Actus Lend Lease, and 4,235 sets of family housing at Fort Campbell were turned over to Actus. The Fort Campbell Family Housing LLC was formed. As the soldier barracks modernization project worked with the Installation Real Property Planning Board to develop brigade footprints, so, too, did the planning board partner with Actus to develop an installation plan for revitalized neighborhood communities as the old housing areas were renovated and the new housing areas were built. The concept that drove the neighborhood community theme was called by architects and city planners the "New Urbanism." The concept of New Urbanism advocated for neighborhoods with diverse populations centered on public spaces and community institutions that would be pedestrian friendly and consist of architecture and landscape that

An artist's rendering of the New Urbanism–style housing and neighborhood.

celebrated local history, climate, ecology and building practices.[70] Actus designers integrated community center facilities in the neighborhoods, and the Installation Real Property Planning Board worked with Actus, MWR, the school system and other stakeholders to integrate health and dental clinics, shoppettes, an elementary school (Barsanti) and recreational areas as part of an overall community plan. If past is prologue, and if one would appreciate the irony, the neighborhood environment and proximity to services of the New Urbanism looked a lot, in concept anyway, like the neighborhood that developed around the old Splinter Village of 1952, even without the benefit of an architectural theory.

CHAPTER 9

CIVITAS!

Civitas: Latin for "the city." The idea and the necessity of a city for the safety, security and flourishing of people is nearly as old as western civilization itself. In 350 BC, the Greek philosopher Aristotle wrote, "When several villages are united in a single, complete community, large enough to be nearly or quite self-sufficing, the city comes into existence, originating in the bare needs of life, and continuing in existence for the sake of the good life."

The decision made in that summer of 1941 to survey for an armor camp somewhere between Hopkinsville and Clarksville was made in order to select a place. A very good place was selected. Power, water, labor, transportation infrastructure, a supportive population, terrain and climate—these things made for a very good place. But a city is not just a place. If it were just a place, it would be nothing more than a group habitat. A city is also defined by its people and its purpose. A city is a combination of place, people and purpose.

This place, so well chosen, proved adaptable to its changing purpose. One can visualize how the place was adapted to fit its new purpose by imagining a map of the pre-camp terrain upon which one could overlay a construction template of each era of the city's history. Each successive layer would reveal an architectural progression from the original curvilinear design of the World War II mobilization camp to the New Urbanism design of today. Successive layers would reveal the transition from a giant bachelor city to a newer kind of world-class Army home city capable of supporting Army families. Each successive layer would also reveal the changing military purpose. Cold War nuclear facilities; airborne drop zones; complex air assault training ranges;

rail, air and line haul facilities to support expeditionary warfare; and the facilities that support special operations unit training would all be part of that evolving template.

It is still possible to visualize the changing purpose of the city today from ground level by driving along the streets of the old spine of the original cantonment: Tennessee, Kentucky and Indiana Avenues. Now, and for a few more years to come, one can catch in one view the unique architecture of every era of the city's history. That visual experience will be gone soon enough as the World War II wood and the Korean-era brick hammerheads come down. Yet even when those old buildings and facilities are gone and a template of the newer city to come is built over the old, the framework and the skeleton of the original cantonment will still be discernible. If you know your history, you will feel and appreciate it. Gate 4 is still the official entrance to the city, and T-39 still stands proudly at the highest and most central location in the old cantonment.

If there are two lessons to be learned from this story of how Fort Campbell came to be what it is today, the first lesson comes from that famous observation in the book of Ecclesiastes: "There is nothing new under the sun." We, as a nation, work hard to care for our soldiers and their families. Examples go clear back to Martha Washington and Kitty Green knitting socks for the soldiers at Valley Forge. When one digs deeply into the history of the city of Fort Campbell, one gets the sense of how deeply this care for our soldiers is engrained in our national character. When the giant bachelor cities were conceived in those dark days of incremental mobilization, the care of the soldier at a level worthy of his dignity and service was written into the enabling legislation. How we have cared for the soldier and his family has varied from era to era and has been a reflection of the social and cultural context of those eras, but the why has not. It is amazing that for every program or service offered today there is a historical antecedent: "There is nothing new under the sun." Our great school system on the installation today has as its antecedent the makeshift classrooms in the temporary housing of 1948. The modern child development centers of today have an antecedent in the nursery located in the old wards of the Station Hospital. Examples abound. The examples are encouraging. They remind us that we should never lose sight of caring for the soldier and his family, which is a defining characteristic of our civic heritage. We should capitalize on that spirit whenever we can as a means to motivate ourselves to ensure Fort Campbell remains a world-class Army home.

A second lesson that comes from our history as a city is about balance. A proper city is a balance of place, people and purpose. For a military installation, purpose will always be weighted a little more heavily in the equation than place or people. Purpose, when out of balance, could lead to a city becoming too utilitarian. The earliest and most austere days of the 12th Armored Division at Camp Campbell or the years of diverting resources from needed infrastructure development to support the Basic Combat Training Command effort are examples of times when the balance equation may have been pulled a little too far in the direction of purpose. It is likewise possible that balance can go too far in the direction of people. Too much of a pull in the direction of people for services, programs and benefits could lead to an entitlement mentality that would be very destructive to the larger Army value of selfless service. The third leg of the balance equation is that of place. Place can be pulled out of balance too. The congressionally mandated Base Realignment and Closure (BRAC) process is an example of the need to make a judgment to let go of a place, no matter how beloved, when the place no longer serves its purpose.

Keeping the equation of place, people and purpose in balance is a matter of mature judgment and leadership. We expect our senior leaders to make wise judgments. Knowing and appreciating the dynamics of the history of our city can guide them as they make judgments and exercise their leadership to keep our city in balance. The city of Fort Campbell will move forward into its next transformation, whatever that might be. It will adapt to the new circumstances and become the next city of Fort Campbell. Along the way, if we seek to remain a world-class Army home, we should remember Aristotle's injunction about the nature of the civitas once it comes into being: the nature of the city is not just that men live but that men live well.

NOTES

Chapter 1

1. Kreidberg and Henry, *History of Military Mobilization*, 556. For a more detailed discussion, see Conn and Fairchild, *Framework of Hemisphere Defense.*
2. Ibid., 548–50.
3. Ibid., 576.
4. *World War II: Why We Fight*, a series directed by Frank Capra and Anatole Litvak and produced by the Office of War Information between 1942 and 1944, is an excellent example of raw newsreel footage packaged into a documentary and made widely available to the American public.
5. Kriv, ed., *World War II*, 3.
6. Kreidberg and Henry, *History of Military Mobilization*, 574.
7. Kriv, ed., *World War II*, 13.
8. Fine and Remington, *Corps of Engineers*, 387–92; also see McCullough, *Truman*, 256–70.
9. Greenfield, Palmer and Wiley, *Organization of Ground Combat Troops*, 57–72.
10. Kriv, ed., *World War II*, 35.
11. Ibid., 34–36.
12. Ibid., 38–39.
13. Ibid., 44; see endnote 114, 70 for list of the new camps; also see Fine and Remington, *Corps of Engineers*, 344–48.

NOTES

Chapter 2

14. Kreidberg and Henry, *History of Military Mobilization*, 621–25.
15. Kriv, ed., *World War II*, 40; also see Jonas, "Camp Campbell," 9–14.
16. Hart, "History of Fort Campbell," 8; see also *Kentucky New Era*, 28 June 1941.
17. Hart, "History of Fort Campbell," 10.
18. Jonas, "Camp Campbell," 10.
19. *Kentucky New Era*, 17 June and 28 July 1941; *Clarksville Leaf-Chronicle*, 29 July 1941.
20. Kriv, ed., *World War II*, 207, 208.
21. *Clarksville Leaf-Chronicle*, 30 July and 1 August 1941.
22. Ibid., 27 August 1941.
23. Hart, "History of Fort Campbell," 12.
24. *Clarksville Leaf-Chronicle*, 21 August 1941.
25. Ibid., 2 August 1941.
26. Osantowski, *Black Landed Gentry*, 69–84.

Chapter 3

27. Jonas, "Camp Campbell," 40; see also *Clarksville Leaf-Chronicle*, 20 January 1941.
28. Osantowski, *Black Landed Gentry*, 71–74, provides a description of how the court proceedings took place.
29. Jonas, "Camp Campbell," 47.
30. *Clarksville Leaf-Chronicle*, 26 January and 31 January 1942.
31. Jonas, "Camp Campbell," 46–53; see also *Clarksville Leaf-Chronicle*, 29 January, 27 February, 24 April and 14 May 1942.
32. *Clarksville Leaf-Chronicle*, 30 March 1942; Hart, "History of Fort Campbell," 18.
33. The names of the six towns were Parker Town, Weaver Store, Rose Hill, Jordan Springs, Asbury and Big Meadow.

Chapter 4

34. Greenfield, Palmer and Wiley, *Organization of Ground Combat Troops*, 498.
35. Hart, "History of Fort Campbell," 38–40.
36. Millet, *Organization and Role*, 313–37.

37. Sloan, *With the Second Army.*
38. *20ᵗʰ Armored Division*, 11.

Chapter 5

39. Chanchani, "Historic Context," 40.
40. Stuart, *Creating the National Security State.*
41. Carlson, *From Cottage to Work Station.*
42. James Hurst, oral history interview, Pratt Museum Archives, Clarksville Base Collection.
43. Bacevich, *Pentomic Era.*
44. "Historic Context for Capehart Wherry Housing."
45. Jaeger and Pearson, "History of Fort Campbell," 44.
46. Baldwin, "Four Housing Privatization Programs," 15–16.
47. Harrington, "Impact Aid."
48. Jaeger and Pearson, "History of Fort Campbell," 130.
49. *Officer's Guide*, 233–35.
50. Jaeger and Pearson, "History of Fort Campbell," 137.
51. Ibid., 132; see "Anatomy of Operation Overdrive," 176.

Chapter 6

52. Hart, "History of Fort Campbell," 96; see "History of the 6ᵗʰ Infantry Division."
53. Hart, "History of Fort Campbell," 100.
54. "History of the Combat Arms Group."
55. Moreau, *Waiting Wives.*
56. Hart, "History of Fort Campbell," 113; see 101ˢᵗ Airborne Division (Airmobile), Annual Historical Summary, CY 1972, 9–10.

Chapter 7

57. Scales, *Certain Victory*, 6–7.
58. Ibid., 36. For a detailed discussion of the doctrinal component of the AOE initiative, see Romjue, *Army of Excellence.*
59. For example, see *Life*, "Bill Mauldin's Willie and Joe."

60. Hart, "History of Fort Campbell," 127.

61. Ibid., 121–23.

62. Chanchani, "Historic Context," 69.

63. Scales, *Certain Victory*, 36.

64. Lippard, "101st Airborne Division," 4.

65. Ibid., 5.

66. Muller, Hutchinson and Goldstone, "Economic Impacts," i–v.

67. Fontenot, Degan and Tohn, *On Point*, 4–5.

68. Page, "Brief History of the 101st Airborne Division," 4.

CHAPTER 8

69. "Army Barracks Master Plan," v.

70. Godfrey and Sadin, "History of the U.S. Army's Residential Communities Initiative," 75–76.

BIBLIOGRAPHY

NEWSPAPERS

Clarksville Leaf-Chronicle, Clarksville, Tennessee, August 1941–present
Defender, Fort Campbell, Kentucky, June 1966–April 1972
Fort Campbell Courier, Fort Campbell, Kentucky, September 1950–present
Kentucky New Era, Hopkinsville, Kentucky, June 1941–present
Retreat to Taps, Fort Campbell, Kentucky, September 1943–1 July 1944

BOOKS

Bacevich, Andrew J. *The Pentomic Era: The U.S. Army Between Korea and Vietnam.* Washington, D.C.: National Defense Press, 1986.
Camp Campbell, Kentucky. Nashville, TN: C.P. Clark, Inc., 1943.
Carlson, Allan C. *From Cottage to Work Station: The Family's Search for Social Harmony in the Industrial Age.* San Francisco: Ignatius Press, 1993.
Carter, Captain Joseph. The *History of the 14ᵗʰ Armored Division.* 1946. Reprint, Evansville, IN: UNIGRAPHIC, INC., 1977.
Conn, Stetson, and Byron Fairchild. *The Framework for Hemisphere Defense.* The United States Army in World War II. The Western Hemisphere. Washington, D.C.: Office of the Chief of Military History, 1960.
Conn, Stetson, Rose Engelman and Byron Fairchild. *Guarding the United States and Its Outposts.* The United States Army in World War II. The

Western Hemisphere. Washington, D.C.: Office of the Chief of Military History, 1964.

Fine, Lenore, and Jesse Remington. *The Corps of Engineers: Construction in the United States.* The United States Army in World War II. The Technical Services. Washington, D.C.: Office of the Chief of Military History, 1972.

Fontenot, Colonel Gregory, Colonel E.J. Degan and Lieutenant Colonel David Tohn. *On Point: The United States Army in Operation Iraqi Freedom.* Vol. 1, *Through 01 May 2003.* Fort Leavenworth, KS: Combat Studies Institute Press, 2004.

Gaddis, John Lewis. *Strategies of Containment: A Critical Appraisal of Postwar American National Security Policy.* New York: Oxford University Press, 1982.

Greenfield, Kent, Robert Palmer and Bell Wiley. *The Organization of Ground Combat Troops.* United States Army in World War II. The Army Ground Forces. Washington, D.C.: Historical Division Department of the Army, 1947.

The Hellcats in World War II: A History of the United States Twelfth Armored Division 15 September, 1942–17 December, 1945. 1946. Reprint, Nashville, TN: Battery Press, 1978.

Kreidberg, Marvin A., and Merton G. Henry. *History of Military Mobilization in the United States Army, 1775–1945.* Department of the Army Pamphlet 20-212, 1955.

Kriv, Arlene R., ed. *World War II and the U.S. Mobilization Program: A History of 700 and 800 Series Cantonment Construction.* Legacy Management Program Department of Defense, 1992.

Lerwill, Leonard L. *The Personnel Replacement System in the United States Army.* Department of the Army Pamphlet 20-211. Washington, D.C.: Office of the Chief of Military History, 1954.

McCullough, David. *Truman.* New York: Simon and Schuster, 1993.

Millet, John. *The Organization and Role of the Army Service Forces.* The United States Army in World War II. The Army Service Forces. Washington, D.C.: Office of the Chief of Military History, 1954.

Moreau, Donna. *Waiting Wives: The Story of Schilling Manor, Home Front to the Vietnam War.* New York: Atria Books, 2005.

Officer's Guide, 20th Edition. Harrisburg, PA: Military Service Publishing Company, 1954.

Osantowski, Teddy Brodie. *The Black Landed Gentry of Montgomery County.* Bloomington, IN: Author House, 2004.

Palmer, Robert, Bell Wiley and William Keast. *The Procurement and Training of Ground Combat Troops.* The United States Army in World War II. Army

Ground Forces. Washington, D.C.: Historical Division Department of the Army, 1948.

Romjue, John. *The Army of Excellence: The Development of the 1980s Army.* TRADOC Historical Monograph Series. Fort Monroe, VA: Historical Office, HQ TRADOC, 1997.

Scales, Robert H. *Certain Victory.* United States Army in the Gulf War. Washington, D.C.: Office of the Chief of Staff, 1993.

Schwarzkopf, General Norman. *It Doesn't Take a Hero: The Autobiography.* New York: Linda Grey Bantam Books, 1992.

Shea, Nancy. *The Waacs.* New York: Harper & Brothers Publishers, 1943.

Sloan, Gene H. *With Second Army Somewhere in Tennessee.* Reprint, n.p., n.d.

Sparrow, John C. *History of Personnel Demobilization in the United States Army.* Department of the Army Pamphlet 26-210, Washington, D.C., 1952.

Stuart, Douglas T. *Creating the National Security State: A History of the Law That Transformed America.* Princeton, NJ: Princeton University Press, 2008.

Taylor, Thomas. *Lightning in the Storm: The 101st Air Assault Division in the Gulf War.* New York: Hippocrene Books, 1994.

Treadwell, Mattie. *The Women's Army Corps.* The United States Army in World War II. Special Studies. Washington, D.C.: Office of the Chief of Military History, 1954.

20th Armored Division in World War II. 1946. Reprint, Marceline, MO: Walsworth Publishing Company, Inc., 1993.

The XX Corps: Its History and Service in World War II. 1946. Reprint, Halstead, KS: W.E.B.S., Inc., 1984.

ARTICLES AND REPORTS

"Army Barracks Master Plan Fiscal Year 2004." Department of the Army, Facilities and Housing Directorate, Office of the Assistant Chief of Staff for Installation Management, July 2004.

Baldwin, William C. "Four Housing Privatization Programs: A History of the Wherry, Capehart, Section 801 and Section 802 Family Housing Programs in the Army." U.S. Army Corps of Engineers, History Office, 1996.

Bellafaire, Judith A. "The Women's Army Corps: A Commemorative of World War II Service." Center for Military History Publication 72-15.

Chanchani, Samiran. "The Historic Context for the Cold War at Ft. Campbell." Submitted to USACE Louisville District by BHE Environmental, Inc., Cincinnati, OH, 2006.

Godfrey, Matthew C., and Paul Sadin. "A History of the U.S. Army's Residential Communities Initiative, 1995–2010." Washington, D.C.: Government Printing Office, 2012.

Harrington, Carolyn D. "Impact Aid, Public Laws 815 and 874, Encyclopedia of Education, 2002." Encyclopedia.com (accessed 3 August 2004), www.encyclopdia.com/doc/1G2-3403200310.html.

"Historic Context for Capehart Wherry Housing." Abstract (accessed 2 August 2014), achp.gov/army-capefartwherry.html.

Life. "Bill Mauldin's Willie and Joe Look at the New Army." February 5, 1971.

Lippard, Clifford M., 1LT. "101st Airborne Division (Air Assault) Operations Desert Shield/Desert Storm Command Report." Fort Campbell, KY, 1 July 1991, 4.

Muller, Thomas, Richard A. Hutchinson and Debra Goldstone. "The Economic Impacts of Desert Shield/Desert Storm Deployments on Local Communities." Bethesda, MD: Logistics Management Institute, February 1992.

THESES, DISSERTATIONS AND UNPUBLISHED MANUSCRIPTS

"Anatomy of Operation Overdrive." Fort Campbell, Kentucky, 1960.

Fisher, Shawn A. "The Battle of Little Rock." PhD diss., University of Memphis, 2013.

Hart, Kevin. "A History of Fort Campbell, Kentucky 1942–1978." Master's thesis, Austin Peay State University, 1979.

"History of the Combat Arms Group, July 1968 to July 1969." N.p., n.d.

HQ 6th Infantry Division. "History of the 6th Infantry Division, 24 November 1967 to 25 July 1968." N.p., n.d.

Jaeger, Lieutenant John, and Lieutenant David Pearson. "History of Fort Campbell, Kentucky." N.p., n.d.

Jonas, Clyde L. "Camp Campbell, Kentucky: A History of Construction and Occupation During World War II." Unpublished master's thesis, Austin Peay State University, 1973.

Moser, Captain John. "A History of Fort Campbell, Kentucky." Fort Campbell, KY: Public Information Office, 1952.

Page, Captain James. "A Brief History of the 101st Airborne Division (Air Assault) in Operation Iraqi Freedom from 19 March 2003 to 06 February 2004." Fort Campbell, KY, 2007.

"Red Devils in Japan: 1955–1956." N.p., n.d.

INDEX

INDEX

S

Sandia Laboratories 117
Selective Service Act 27
Senate Special Committee to
      Investigate the National Defense
      Program 28
700 Series Plan 30
Skilled, Tough, Ready to go Around the
      Clock (STRAC) 111
Somervell, Brigadier General Brehon
      33, 35, 39, 74
special operations units 162
Special Services Branch 84, 96, 102,
      110, 139, 141
Strategic Air Command (SAC) 112,
      118
Strategic Army Force 150

T

Taylor, Colonel Herbert E. 77
Tennessee-Kentucky Armor Camp 13,
      16, 33, 34, 39, 47, 67, 70, 90
Tennessee Maneuver Area 78
Terrell, Major General Henry 89
town hall meetings 158
transient housing 129
Truman, Senator Harry 28

U

United States Army Reception Station
      149
U.S. Army Nurse Corps 96

V

volunteer Army (VOLAR) 155

W

Wagner Act 63
waiting wives 152
Walker, Lieutenant General Walton 87
Week of the Eagles 156
Wherry, Senator Kenneth S. 131

Willkie, Wendell 32
Wilson, Bell & Watkins 39, 42
Women's Army Corps (WAC) 98
Women's Auxiliary Army Corps
      (WAAC) 97
Wysong, Captain Kenneth 48

Z

Zebra Club 140

ABOUT THE AUTHOR

John J. O'Brien retired from a twenty-year active-duty military career as a lieutenant colonel of infantry. He is currently an Army historian assigned as the installation historian at Fort Campbell, Kentucky. He is a graduate of the University of San Francisco, BA in government; Lincoln University, MA in political science; the Command and General Staff College and School of Advanced Military Studies, MMAS in military theory and history; and is a doctoral candidate in U.S. history at Saint Louis University. In addition to his Army duties at Fort Campbell, he is an adjunct member of the History and Philosophy Department at Austin Peay State University, where he teaches introductory U.S. history and directs a senior internship in public history. He resides happily with his family on a small farm in Christian County, Kentucky.